MW00354167

Confessions of a Mystic Soccer Mom

A Life Played With Feet in Both Worlds

Also by Monica

My Karma Ran Over My Dogma:
Lessons Learned by a Whistle Blowing Minister
Turned Mystic

You are Light:
8 Words Reveal Your Truest Self

Confessions of a Mystic Soccer Mom

A Life Played With Feet in Both Worlds

Monica McDowell

SYNCLECTIC MEDIA

Copyright © 2012 by Monica McDowell, MDiv

All rights reserved. This book may not be reproduced in whole or in part, stored in a retrieval system, or transmitted in any form or by any means electronic, mechanical, or other without written permission from the author, except by a reviewer, who may quote brief passages in a review.

Details of clients and their stories have been altered for confidentiality.

Published by **Synclectic Media**
Seattle, Washington
www.synclectic.com

Publisher's Cataloging-in-Publication Data

McDowell, Monica
  Confessions of a Mystic Soccer Mom: a life played with feet in both worlds / Monica McDowell. – 1st ed.
    p. cm. –
  Summary: Set half at the hearth and half in heaven, Confessions is a riveting read that will inspire women to reclaim their sacred feminine power by daring to weave the extraordinary into the everyday of their own lives.

  Library of Congress Control Number: 2012935765
  ISBN: 9780615587608

                                                              P-CIP

---

10 9 8 7 6 5 4 3 2 1

Ω
First Edition
Printed in the United States

Dedicated to my mom and grandmothers
~Sarah, Olive, and Rachel~

May all of the voices and songs of our hearts be heard

10% of the publisher's proceeds from
Confessions of a Mystic Soccer Mom will be donated to
Heifer International.
www.heifer.org

Contents

Turtle Totem

Introduction:
The Mundane, the Sacred, and a Crow

The iconic soccer mom. Or hockey mom. Or "whatever" mom. No matter how you define the "whatever," you know this woman. If you're a mom it's because you most likely are her, or have been her. If you're not a mom, it's because you've inevitably seen her. Hint: She's the one who before school, after school, evenings, and weekends is schlepping the fruit of her loin around town to sports, music, drama, and social events. She spends a gazillion hours a week doing this, because her CTV (child transportation vehicle) is her absolute favorite place to be in the whole wide world.

Ahem.

Anyway, I know this woman because, I confess, I am her, too. Even though, for reasons known only to the gods and goddesses of athletics (Nike, *et al*), my children have participated in every sport known to humankind *but* soccer, in every other respect I fit the archetype of the so-called soccer mom—

Except, I add another word to the front of my societal title: mystic.

You may be wondering, though, how the word mystic could even be used in the same sentence with "soccer mom" let alone, as its sole descriptor. If so, good thinking! For how *could* a mystic possibly live her life as a veritable soccer mom, with her feet firmly entrenched in both the worlds of heaven and hearth? Isn't the contemplative life reserved for monks and nuns, yogis and hermits, cloistered far away from everything having to do with motherhood? For centuries, this indeed has been the path—mom or mystic: choose.

Nonetheless, I have increasing evidence nowadays that more is lurking behind the chauffeuring, chef, and chaperoning roles that mothers everywhere play, confirming for me that I am far from destined to stay on the sidelines of societal mommyhood in my spirituality. At a track meet last spring, I overheard one bona fide soccer mom tell another, "You know my friend, Susie? She told me she meditates every morning for twenty minutes, emptying her mind of all thoughts. It helps her get through the day. I need to try that."

Yet another mom confided in me, "The other day, I saw these baby birds that had fallen out of their nest. I started praying 'God, help those baby birds' like I thought I was gall-darned St. Francis of Assisi or something and I thought, *What is going on with me?*"

So I know I'm not the only mother in the world seeking the more that masquerades in and through and around the mundane. In fact, I am beginning to suspect that perhaps there is a movement underway—a movement that millions of women feel deep down in their embodied souls that has yet to be publicly affirmed because of fears of being labeled crazy, medieval, or god-forbid, heretical.

I, however, am happy to christen myself a mad domestic goddess. It has set me free to enjoy the miraculous in my everyday life. Just a few days ago, I was on my daily, routine walk about the neighborhood when the unexpected happened. A crow—an ordinary, black, garden-variety crow—allowed me to get very close to it before it took off in flight from the ground. As it lifted into the air, our energies must have merged because I felt, visceral and real, the sensation of the flapping of wings in my own shoulders, as if I were the one transcending the laws of gravity. I stopped in my tracks, spellbound by this brief ascension into the mystery of winged existence.

It reminded me, "There are no ordinary moments," as Dan Millman, author of *The Way of the Peaceful Warrior*, says. Truly, all around us the sacred is breaking into existence, even into the most monotonous tasks of life. If I can find a divine message waiting for me as I clean the counter under my microwave (*Yuk! How long has it been since I last did this? Hmmm. How long has it been since I last ventured into the unseen muck in my own soul for some deep-cleaning there?*), I know significance is ever present.

After years of living this mystical mothering, it is my firm belief that the universe loves to throw spontaneous surprise parties for each of us—the Beloved's way of winking at us from behind the veil. All that is needed for me, for any mom, or for *anyone* for that matter, is to merely to be open—open to the wonder, the magic, the miraculous that can greet you with a Gomer Pyle-esque "Suuur-priiise!" in any moment of any day.

My hope is that the reflections in this book will help you do just that: learn to stay open to the extraordinary amidst the everyday. Journey with me as my ordinary life is interrupted by the mystical again and again. I know there is vastly more than meets the eye in your world, too. May the words within this book inspire all of you as women, whether birthers, midwives, mothers, leaders, or healers, to reclaim your spiritual power as you bring the sacred into being. It's not just for monks anymore.

Both your feet are waiting.

Questions for Reflection: How has Spirit gotten your attention lately? How do you birth the sacred into being in your own life already?

Part One
~Of Females and the Feminine~

Lovin' my German, Non-Yoga Body

Don't get me wrong. I like yoga and do a few yoga poses daily. But keep in mind that yoga began, not in northern Europe with Nordic-Slavic-Germanic female body types like mine, but in India, with thin-limbed, near anorexic-looking, southern Asian, male body types. In other words, large breasts and thick thighs prevent an accurate presentation of a good number of yoga poses and if you think otherwise, you don't have large breasts and thick thighs. Trust me. I'm naturally very flexible and even when I was marathon lean, my mammaries got in the way of fluid transitions to new poses and my hamstring-quadriceps combo were far from yoga lithe.

I've learned not to do negative self-talk around this but to accept that yoga isn't my path to body awareness. It's simply a helpful stretching tool. When it works—great. When it doesn't—no big deal. My personal path to body awareness and body-love has been a messier one: motherhood. If you've gestated, birthed, and lactated for five and a half years like I have, or even if your motherhood came post-birth through fostering or adopting and you had to clean up the myriad bodily secretions that spout continually from the gamut of a baby's orifices, you know what I mean. When you're in full mommy mode, you cannot ignore the body—you cannot escape flesh and blood. You can dislike it and even hate it, but you cannot escape it. The path to liberation for me was accepting and even embracing my body and the precious bodyfruits of my womb.

As a mystic mom then, this body-love isn't about seeing everything as illusion and trying to escape into a blissed-out nirvana, Shangri-la, or heaven, but embracing that illusion for its beauty, its marvels, its daily miracles that enable transcendent spirit to remain imminently incarnate—the grand marriage of essence and form—able to create a living, breathing infant with all the delight and messiness that means. And my body, *my body*, was the instrument of the Soul's threshold entrance into this material existence, no matter how illusory. I learned, therefore, to praise my body for its excellent strength and wisdom—to love it with all of its being—yoga capable or not and certainly, Hollywood beautiful or not.

It has its complications, to be sure—this wielding and weaving of Spirit into body. As I have experienced the rewiring of my brain and the transformation of my body to be a conduit of healing light, things can go a little, well, haywire. It's not a perfect fit. Spirit as limitless and free, whole and pure must merge with the limited and bounded, the light and the dark. Sometimes a new energy download will splay me out on my bed for a few hours like a filleted flounder. The energy is so powerful my body and brain have to go offline to accommodate the new information, just like a program update needs a computer to reboot to work. Often the energy coming in is so painful, I feel like I'm back in transitional labor sans drugs—a sort of energy rebirthing of my own soul into embodiment at a new level yet again.

I once decided to try a new meditation practice I had read about. A few hours after doing this meditation, my heart started burning in my chest like I had just chugalugged a flaming cocktail. I thought at first it must have been something I ate, but I recalled that I hadn't eaten anything with any inflammatory properties at all. Everything had been bland, really. Then it hit me: I was in the full tide of PMS. Beware, then, the dangers of starting a new meditation practice when the hormones are a little tippy! (Be sure to check out my next book: *Meditation and Mood Swings: Your New PMS Path to Hormonal Hell.*)

So many women have body image issues and I thoroughly understand. It grieves me that our sacred temples, even given the lumps of clay they can resemble *au naturel* (especially in fluorescent lighting), have been so denigrated, so desecrated in our world that we women have a hard time simply thanking our bodies, let alone celebrating, nay, even worshipping them as the transubstantial communion of the Goddess within us all.

Real goddesses have the battle scars to prove it—not medically unnecessary plastic surgery scars or cement-pumped up butts (wait, women actually do that?)—but c-section scars, tubal ligation scars, hysterectomy scars, needle biopsy scars, and breast reconstruction scars. We are battling for our bodies and for the bodies women have birthed, not battling against our bodies. We have labored and nursed and sleep deprived our way into birthing the world—wrinkles, sags, enlarged pores, and cellulite be damned!

Dance, divine Goddess within us! Dance, divine Goddess in our bodies! Dance! Give thanks! We are the god and goddess bearers of the world!

I confess: As a virtual mystic soccer mom I'm dancing with both feet—miracles, messes, and all.

Questions for Reflection: What are you thankful for about your own body? How can you celebrate it today? How has messiness been a teacher for you?

The Rise of the Black Madonna

In the midst of a tumultuous saga[1] (please read the footnote for understanding), I found myself struggling with a non-beneficial, exclusively male image of God, even though many years prior, while attending seminary as a pregnant mom, I had embraced the idea of the Sacred Feminine and God as Divine Mother. During my seminary re-education, I bought a sweatshirt to wear at Yuletide that had a traditional nativity scene displayed on the front—with a bit of a twist. Someone in the nativity scene is pronouncing loudly, "It's a girl!" This sweatshirt has met with laughs, scoffs, astonishment, as well as deep appreciation as I have continued to wear it over the years.

But in the midst of my whistle-blowing years, I was repeatedly running into patriarchy in the church and the good ol' boys club (with even some social justice clergywomen playing into that club) that to an extent, my faith faltered. On one particular day in the midst of the saga, I lamented to God:

Why did the Christ figure in Western history come as a male? I know he obliterated social taboos and stood with women in solidarity in a way a woman messiah could never have even had the opportunity of doing 2000 years ago in that society. I know he is the embodiment of both masculine and feminine attributes and was the incarnation of the Divine Wisdom—the Sophia of God. But why aren't there any women Christ figures? Or even women mystics that are deep in our collective psyche the way Jesus, Buddha, and other "male saviors" are?

I confess: I was really wrestling with this one. It seemed a lot of suffering had impacted so many for such a long time because of this imbalance in our view of a divine man rather than the complementary energy of divine man and divine woman.

That night, I was unable to fall asleep in bed because of damage to my heart's nerve endings. All of the stress of the saga had fried my nerves and the damage often caused my heart's nerves to spark when I tried to go to sleep lying down. Not only was this alarming and excruciating, it was incredibly non-restful, and just as I would start to slip into the dream state, the spasm of a heart spark would wake me straight up. This pattern could go on for hours. Fortunately, through trial and error I found that I could fall asleep much easier if I was sitting up, as somehow it greatly diminished if not eliminated the sparking. The comfiest place to do that in our house was on the cushy sofa in my spiritual healing office in the basement, so the night of my lament, I ventured down the stairs with my pillow and blanket in hand. Upon arriving, I propped myself up on the creamy white sofa, and fell asleep relatively easily.

I don't know why, but a lot of very interesting things happened when I slept on that sofa in my office. This time was no exception.

Early in the morning, just after dawn and sleeping soundly, I awoke as I felt myself pulled out of my body just to the side of the sofa. Whatever was pulled out of my body, the "me of my soul," was pure electric. I perceived I was a sphere of brilliant white—and yet also multi-colored—light, and I felt myself, as this light-essence-being, held in the strong arms that had just pulled me out of my body. These arms then started to rock me gently back and forth, just like a momma would soothe a baby in her arms. This lasted for a little while and then I was put back in my body. As soon as I was back in my body, I opened my eyes and saw a black woman waving at me near the door of my office. She then turned and disappeared.

Intuitively, I felt she was a black female Christ coming in response to my heart-deep struggle to understand God's seeming allowance of predominantly male figures as divinity in the West. A couple of weeks later I was reading something by the author, Sue Monk Kidd. She stated that more and more people are reporting the appearances of the black Madonna. To me it was essentially one and the same, a black female Christ or a black Madonna. I took the visitation as God's answer to my prayer: even though the West and largely the world has associated the Divinity with maleness, Spirit can take any form She or He chooses to make the sacred real and meaningful to us at any time in any way.

So allow God to open your horizons about who God really is. Allow God to shatter your old forms and images that no longer serve Love or your highest and best. Take a step of faith to trust in the God who is pure Unconditional Love for all.

Questions for Reflection: What forms has God taken for you? What form has the most meaning for you right now?

[1] **Note:** Several times in these reflections I refer to "my saga." In a nutshell, during the years 2000-2005, I was a whistle-blowing minister. It began when, as an associate pastor of a church, I reported the sexual misconduct of my supervisor, the senior pastor. This started a series of severe retaliatory actions against me by him, then the church, the denominational higher-ups, and so forth. It escalated into a national event after I filed discrimination lawsuits in 2002. By 2004 I had become the first ordained minister in the country ever granted civil rights by a federal appellate court. This federal ruling was upheld during a revote challenge in 2005, and soon afterward, I settled my case out-of-court and left the denomination.

The road to this legally precedent-setting ruling was a harrowing one, during which my family and I lost nearly everything. However, it was also my path to mystical awakening, and I am so grateful for the multiple blessings that have come my way because of what happened to me during those five fateful years. If you would like to know more, please read my book, *My Karma Ran Over My Dogma: Lessons Learned by a Whistle-Blowing Minister Turned Mystic*. I've included a preface to it at the end of this book to provide a bridge to my overall life story.

Marbles the Miraculous

The outward form of things passes away
but the essence remains forever.
How long will you be in love with the shape of the jug?
Throw aside the jug, and seek the water.
If you look too closely at the form, you miss the essence.
The wise always pick out the pearl from the shell.
    ~Rumi

A while ago I had an unforgettable healing session with an alternative energy healer. In the few months preceding the session, I had been trying to be mindful of the Oneness of all throughout my daily life. In my novice attempts at this, I was noticing some fearful thoughts skirting around the edges of my consciousness, such as, "Good God, in Oneness I'll be annihilated!" Unable to move past the ever-so-slight paranoia I was feeling, I humbly realized I was a hinterland away from mastering the wisdom of the age-old spiritual adage: *to die before you die.*

However, an intriguing event occurred during my healing session, showing me that a seemingly far away truth can in reality be, well, even closer than the nose on one's face. For about halfway through our time together, the healer burnt some myrrh resin and held it right under my—you guessed it—nose. Upon taking the first big whiff of its pungent smoke, inhaling the incense into the depths of my being, a wizened old Buddhist monk in iridescent orange robes instantly appeared to me. The name "Thich Tri Chon" came through.

As incongruous as making small talk right before the Big Bang, the monk commented on the state of my wrists. I was thinking, *Huh?? An old Buddhist monk came all this way to tell me to exercise my wrists more?* But then the monk led me into a spiritual lesson I will never forget. He asked me to become one with something, so I chose the fragrant, sweet-smelling grape hyacinths planted in the front yard of my house. I became one with the flowers energetically and felt the joy of their being and the bliss of oneness with them. (Don't ask me how I did this. I don't know. I just did it.) As soon as I was in this awareness, the monk announced as dryly as a deadpan comedian, "You just died."

Stunned by the simple yet profound nature of this insight, I almost snapped out of my meditative reverie. But like turning a spoonful of luxuriant chocolate mousse over and over again in my mouth, my soul continues to savor the rich depth of this lesson, trying to capture every last bit of its essence. Indeed, I have learned so much. Since this healing session, I've been able to release some lingering fears of dying prematurely from near fatalities I had during my whistle-blowing saga. I also became aware of more attachments to my ego identity I needed to let go of, so I wasn't tied down to my own limited self-image. I've also embraced that I need not dread the deaths of loved ones. Bottom line: when I was in the total awareness of Oneness, I knew—*there is no loss in bliss.*

However, this new understanding was put to the test later that year when our beloved cat, Marbles, passed from form into essence. I grieved more for her than I think I would for many humans. Actually, I wasn't grieving for her—I was grieving for myself. I had attached so much to her, to the *form* of her, I had missed the essence, just like Rumi's poem above warns against. To be sure, Rumi's poem and this reflection are not an indictment against grief or against admiring the beauty of every form the Divine manifests in and through— far from it. It's simply a reminder to see beyond the forms that can so easily seduce us into forgetting the essence of Who is in and through all.

And there is much to admire about the beauty of Marbles' essence. A doting mother cat, she always wanted to go outside when my children did. Then she'd perch on some high, grassy knoll of a neighbor's yard and keep a watchful eye on them as they played. When they'd come home, she'd follow along behind them, making sure they made it safely. If one of us was feeling blue, Marbles would come by and nestle and cuddle until moods brightened. Little girls who lived down the street stopped by and knocked on our door daily just so they could visit with her. When various neighbors walked by our house, if Marbles happened to be outside, she would walk out to the edge of the street to greet them. Upon hearing that she was gone from us, our neighbors and friends, too, grieved: "We will miss her. She was the nicest, friendliest cat we've ever known."

None of this yet reveals her miraculous nature.

During my saga there were nights I didn't think I'd live to see the morning, my heart was so devastated from grief and stress. Yet, Marbles always knew when she was needed, and she would literally lie over my heart on those nights. If my heart's erratic sparks hurt her, she'd yelp, but never did she budge. I believe her phenomenal healings saved my life on more than one occasion. She also regularly participated in energy healing sessions with clients and groups, intuitively knowing who needed a healing touch. With one client, a woman who was abused by her mother, Marbles jumped up beside her and started licking her wrists and face. She knew this client needed a true mother's care. Marbles was an amazing and gifted healer, and I am so grateful for the ever-present, self-giving love she offered freely to all of us, just like the Divine Mother Essence she was, in fact, just a form of.

The week Marbles got sick and died, a seer friend of mine did some work with her helping her cat spirit pass over. When my friend witnessed this eventually happen, she was surprised. Marbles' cat spirit didn't feel like a cat at all to her and so my friend asked her, "Are you really a cat?"

"No!" was the immediate reply.

Then she said Marbles' spirit turned into "like an angel."

Of course. All who met her already knew that on some level.

We have since had much evidence in dreams, signs, and visitations that Marbles is alive and well and still looking out for us from the other side. Her work with us in physical form is done for now. She may return to us in another form, but her essence—the unconditional Mother Love of the Beloved—is always with us, always watching over, ever giving, ever healing, ever loving. Truly there is no loss in bliss, but blasted! I confess: I still miss that cat.

Questions for Reflection: Where does the Mother Love of the Divine show up in your life? What does, "There is no loss in bliss," mean for you?

Tibetan Mandalas and Quilting Bees

The Last Mimzy is one of my all-time favorite mystical family movies—besides *The Whale Rider.* Spoiler alert: Do not read the rest of this paragraph if you want to see the movie first! In the film's plot, a stuffed bunny along with some other "toys" are sent back in time by a scientist in the future in a last-ditched effort to save the planet from ecological disaster. Two siblings in the present time who live in Seattle ("Sweet!"—said in this Seattleite's best *Napoleon Dynamite* voice) find these futuristic toys while vacationing on nearby Whidbey Island. Interacting with these toys gives the children mystical powers: telepathy, telekinesis, higher intelligence, and wait for it—the ability to intuitively understand and mathematically interpret traditional Tibetan mandala designs! Why, of course!

[Here ends my mini-movie review, *The Last Mimzy: Mystical Family Movie Extraordinaire.*]

After seeing this movie and then noticing an announcement that Tibetan monks were going to be demonstrating their spiritual practice of creating mandalas out of sand at a small university near my house, I invited a friend to attend the event along with me. Mandalas, if you don't already know, are symbolic representations of the universe. They are found in almost every spiritual tradition and are typically depicted as a round picture or diagram with varying levels of manifested reality displayed within the circle. A Native American medicine wheel is a type of mandala as is a Celtic labyrinth. Mandalas are often used in meditation and contemplation exercises as well as in therapeutic contexts. Carl Jung, the great psychotherapist, found them to be an excellent healing tool for himself and his clients.

[Here ends my mini-lecture, *Introduction to the Mandala, Spirituality 101.*]

When my friend and I arrived at the university—situated on the vast, park-like grounds of a former Catholic seminary—we made our way through the halls of the first floor to the cafeteria where the monks had set up for their mandala-making. We decided to grab some lunch while we were there, as the university is known for its delicious, organic, vegetarian fare. After we served ourselves heaping portions of lentil soup, brown rice, green salad, and assorted nosh, we carried our trays over to a corner table near the monks. That way we could eat and watch them at the same time.

The process was fascinating.

There were four monks dressed in traditional Tibetan garb and each clearly had a section of the mandala to work on or a specific task to help another monk with his work. The brightly dyed sands were set around in bowls on the large square table-like platform the five-foot by five-foot mandala was being created on. Various sizes of handmade metal funnels, called *chakpur*, were used for pouring sand onto the mandala. Which funnel was used depended on the amount and speed the monk needed the sand to flow. With the switch of a tool or a tilt of the hand, a monk could slow the flow down to a few grains of colored sand at a time for specific placing. They clearly had a design memorized and were filling in the colors as designated by tradition—a kind of extreme color-by-number mandala!

All of this was done in total silence with intense looks of concentration in the tightened brows of each monk. After awhile we could see the painstaking attention to detail taught the monks mental focus—a type of active meditation. We watched for a good hour, and then left when the bold color combinations began to wear on our eyes. Of course, as is tradition, when the sand mandala was finished in a couple of days it would be completely dismantled. I knew this was to symbolize the Buddhist teaching of impermanence: Everything is passing; everything is temporal; all forms are created and then destroyed in a never-ending cycle of samsara.

After I contemplated this when I was back home, a voice rose up from within me. She sounded strong. She also sounded, I confess, a bit testy:

Now why are Tibetan monks and not nuns the ones traveling around? And why is this spiritual practice only done by men? And why is an intricate art form considered an internationally renowned spiritual practice when a group of men do it but not so much when a group of women do it, such as, a quilting bee? And why is it considered spiritually profound to destroy an art form? If women destroyed their quilts after they made them, they'd be accused of being frivolous, or worse, wasteful. Anyway, women wouldn't destroy their quilts because quilts are practical and provide services—they keep people warm, they decorate walls, and they recycle scraps of fabric.

Well, well, well, snark much, Monica?

Although my feminist rant has some very valid and important points, upon reflecting further I realized this is more of a case of "intentions matter." In a quilting bee, women are not necessarily setting intentions to meditate and do a spiritual practice. It seems to me they could set out to do so, especially if they did their collective quilting in silence. But more often than not, even though the quilts are sometimes used for service to the greater community, quilting bees are primarily social events.

Nevertheless, as a woman, I am so grateful for movies like *The Last Mimzy* and *The Whale Rider* that emphasize the gift of sacred leadership and even communal salvation coming through females and even girls. I believe Spirit has an intention to rebalance masculine and feminine energies in our world. This will require more art, more stories, more films, and more leadership from women in the public's eye. It means women will need to take more risks, not to do things the way men do them or the way society wants them done, but the way Spirit is directing women to do them. It will require women to step out without fear that their voices will be hushed, their intuition mocked, their bodies desecrated, their authority denied. There are too many of us this time to be hunted down and persecuted back into silence.

If Spirit intends for feminine energies to rise up and for women to call forth a new community of cooperation between women and men, it shall be done. It shall be done indeed.

[Here ends my mini-sermon *Rise Up, Ye Women, Rise Up!*]

Questions for Reflection: What are your favorite female-centered movies or books? How is Spirit calling you to speak your truth and express your creativity more in the world? How can you support and learn from women who are your role models in these areas?

Polka Dot Perceptions and Pekingese Portals

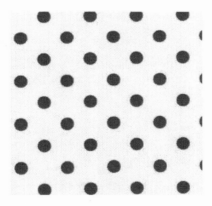

The third eye: that oft sought-after ability in the psychic world. My own third eye has a mind all its own. I have yet to learn to manage what it sees. Maybe that will come in time. When it first reared its other-worldly abilities, I was in the middle of my whistle-blowing saga as well as in the middle of wondering about my sanity, with many strange happenings occurring multiple times a day and night for years.

For example, many nights I would awaken for my three a.m. watering ritual, a routine that began during my first pregnancy and continues to occur nightly nearly two decades later—just one of the many side benefits of having your body taken over by another being. Anyway, as I would get out of bed and saunter over to the bathroom, it was like a movie projector would suddenly flip on inside my head. This internal movie projector would then project film-like images onto an invisible screen about five feet high by four feet wide that was about three feet in front of me. In this live action screen, I could see people doing a variety of different things in various parts of the world. I would also witness images of scenes that were clearly not of this planet. Was I seeing alien life? Or other dimensions and universes? I still don't know.

These live action dramas were not just images, though. They had real, palpable energy and I felt pulled toward them. I believe that if I had known what I was doing, I could have actually stepped into these images and experienced myself in a different place. Is this how bilocation happens? Perhaps. I was too freaked out at the time to allow myself to experiment with sending myself to another time, place, or planet, let alone universe, and so I resisted—hard. Gritting my teeth, clenching my jaw, tensing my thighs and pushing backward against a sumo-sized, invisible force pulling me into these images, I would stand my ground until the sucking force left. Then I would jump back into bed, scrunch my eyes closed tight, make the sign of the cross over me, and recite about a hundred Hail Marys—fast. And I'm not even Catholic.

Since the time my third eye first burst open with such sci-fi-ish drama, nowadays, I usually experience a much less extreme third eye, though sci-fi still seems an apropos adjective. Quite often my third eye appears to open after my awareness travels through a worm-hole-like tunnel, ala *Star Trek*. Other times it just opens and I can see out of my third eye, my inner eye, and my physical eyes all at the same time. And because I'm clearly watching all of these eyes with yet another eye, which I call the Divine eye/I, the third eye really can't be "the be all to end all." It looks like I might have, at last count, five eyes, not counting my glasses. Don't expect me to explain any of this. I confess: I cannot.

The visions, images, and symbols I see through my third eye are often randomly unassociated with anything else—just a stream of visual consciousness. Early one morning when it was still dark outside, I awoke with my third eye open and visions of polka dots dancing in front of me. As I watched the pretty parade of pastels in various patterns morph and merge into each other, all of a sudden, white furry Pekingese puppies popped into view. After pondering these images for a while, I fell back asleep.

When I woke up, my polka dot and Pekingese puppy ponderings were still with me. *Why, of all the images it could send me, would the universe send me such girlish images?* And then, I thought, *Well, why not? We have such male or even adult images of God. What about God as a little girl who enjoys polka dots and Pekingese puppies? Why does all our spirituality have to be so serious?* I love that God as little girl relishes all sorts of silly and pretty and fluffy and cute. I mean God created bunnies and many types of adorable, hilarious animals for us to enjoy.

Perhaps, too, the girlish images showing up in my third eye were a bit of a hint from the universe to lighten up. I confess: I tend to forget to play. Just the other day I was on serious overload—not too much stress, mind you—too much serious. I was feeling about as playful as roadkill. So I meditated, got in touch with my inner fun, and went out for a walk. As I started out I said to the universe in my mind, with as much spunky energy as I could muster, *Okay, I know Nature is naturally playful. Show me what you got.* As I rounded the bend a block away, a huge bald eagle, perched on a low-lying branch of an evergreen on the other side of the road from me, flew out from its hiding spot right towards me. It got within a foot of my head, and then flew up and away. I laughed, as it didn't feel menacing at all—much more like when my cat hides and then jumps out at me to surprise me. A neighbor who was out in his yard and saw the whole thing said in astonishment, "It looked like that eagle was flying *to* you."

I replied with a girlish grin, "I think it was!"

Questions for Reflection: What would it mean to you to envision God as a little girl, brimful of feminine giggles?

The Anti-Martha
(like the Anti-Christ—only better!)

Lately, I've begun dreaming other peoples' dreams. If I touch them, sit in their seat after them, or simply bump into them, I pick up enough of their energy that I dream their dreams at night. These nighttime meanderings are full of people I don't know, their unresolved issues, and places unfamiliar. It's a strange feeling—having someone else's dreams. I see the underside of their understanding of the world, and quite frankly, it's bizarre. I confess: I'm sure it means I'm effing up somewhere on my boundaries.

I recently saw a client who is a Martha Stewart wannabe, Goddess bless her. This client feels a lot of pressure to be perfect in the householding realm of life and after our work together, I had Martha Stewart dreams all night long. This was a first as I am the anti-Martha—known for long lapses of householding duties that inevitably lead to the house hitting bottom harder than an alcoholic after a three-week binge. Co-dependently in denial all the way along, I will suddenly look around and declare with a cluelessness that surpasses the blondest of us all: *How in the world did this house come to look like the Tasmanian Devil on speed took up residence here?* It's probably also the first time the universe has ever given me a client who does not reflect back to me my own issues.

The Martha Stewart dreams I had that night after seeing my client were full of images of an unknown house with myriads of unfamiliar people gathered there for a holiday party. It was all rather wearisome. I felt so much compassion for my client, the hostess, as she seemed set up to fail. She kept trying to do too much to impress, even memorializing her mother in paper cutouts for the holiday decorations.

Ahhh! Trying to please her mom!

Oh wait. Maybe I do have that issue.

A bit.

Maybe.

Anyway, at least it wasn't a nightmare—well, in the sense of having to help your family survive a sudden tsunami flooding the neighborhood or suddenly finding oneself naked in front of an audience—more typical fare for my psyche's fears. I was feeling a bit mentally tortured, though, as I kept observing the great effort the woman in the dream would go through to make everyone happy and make everything look perfect and think to myself, *Really? REALLY??* Then I woke up to the sound of my cat puking. I looked over the edge of the bed to see her producing a putrid orange stain on my beige bedroom carpet. And I thought, *Really? REALLY??*

I may be no banner for householding perfection (in college when I told my mom over the phone I had landed a housekeeping job, she had to hang up because she couldn't stop laughing), but even I don't like cat barf stains on my carpeting. *Sigh.* At least our house is a rental. However, we women need to move past trying to emulate the false images (read: idols) of female perfection, be that Martha Stewart (who is single, whose daughter is grown, who has employed a huge *staff* to help her create her "simple" creations), or be that the photo-shopped women and houses in magazines. The best way I can think of to stop buying into it is to stop buying it—literally. If you do not support the false images (read: idols) of women and houses, don't buy the magazines or the products that promote such images. If women stop buying, the cycle will stop. We are the ones perpetuating the false images!

I laughed heartily at several issues of a popular home and garden magazine that my husband got me as a free trial when he re-subscribed to his woodworking magazine. In one issue, they were trying to promote a simple lifestyle. They had a woman dressed "simply" wearing a $200 shirt, a $100 necklace, a $70 skirt, and $120 shoes, for a whoppingly simple outfit of $495, not counting leggings, rings, and earrings. This advertorial was next to recipes for a simple dinner that "only took three hours to make." [Insert head butt against brick wall here.] Needless to say, I will not be subscribing to their magazine and will at some point tell them why.

This idea that women can do it all is a myth. Even Thoreau couldn't make it in nature all by himself like he so proudly proclaimed. What is not well known was that while he was relying on his so-called self-sufficiency in the idyllic wild, his mother and sisters regularly brought him food and collected his laundry. Excuse me while I blow my nose with a few pages of *On Walden Pond*.

However, the myth that one woman can keep the house clean, the kids decent, the food nutritious, the school volunteered at, the husband happy in bed, and any of her own work done besides has only been a recent invention. Out on the farms of yesteryear there were many helping hands. In numerous cultures there are many women in one household. They may not be liberated in our sense of the word, but how liberated are we if we're strung out on Xanax because we think we should be able to do it all, all by our lone selves, and in the manner of the impossible Martha Stewart picture perfect world?

Remember this when you are trying to do too much to please others or to please your own internalized expectations from society. Remember this when you are lamenting your dirty house or kids. Remember this when you have to run to the store in unwashed hair because you haven't had time for a shower that day. Remember you are not alone. Ever.

You are a wonderful spiritual being worthy of creating space for yourself, worthy of kindness, worthy of so much more than picture perfect perfection. You are worthy of Life, lived in the ever present now, as harried as it may be. You are worthy of joy—the kind that comes from living your own dreams (not others' dreams, picked up intuitively or not!) to create a better world for yourself, for other women, for your family and children, and for all families and children.

You are worthy of Love.

Questions for Reflection: What are expectations you have picked up from other people that are not serving your highest and best? What will it take to let go of those expectations? What are your dreams to contribute more love, joy, and peace to your life and the life of the world?

Part Two
~Of Heaven and Bliss~

Why I Write: The Call[1]

In mid-January of 2008, an unexpected visitor dropped by my house one evening: God.

It was about 7 p.m., and I was relishing a rare triple treat: the house was clean, the dishwasher was humming as it rinsed away our dinner's crumbs, and my children were studiously finishing their homework. All was well. To make the most of it, I scurried off to my bedroom for a much needed mom rest. Stretching out on my bed, I sunk my body into the comforting depths of the downy covers, and started breathing rhythmically and mindfully—one of my favorite ways to practice some good old-fashioned self-care.

All of a sudden, hot molten energy started running from the top of my head to the bottom of my tailbone, over and over again, completely obliterating the myth that lightning never strikes in the same place twice.

Uh-oh. Now what? I said to myself.

Mystical experiences are hardly a new thing for me. I began having them in dump truck loads during my years as a whistle-blowing clergywoman. (See *My Karma Ran Over My Dogma,* for the particulars on that humdinger of a saga.) But this experience was especially unique, not just because of the intensity of the energy surging down my spine, but also because of what occurred next.

While I lay there, I kept my eyes closed and with the fierce concentration of a lioness willed myself not to spontaneously combust in a fiery cremation (as if I had any control at all over what was happening to me...ha!). After a while—I don't know how long as time usually stands still during these experiences—I started wondering when the searing of my nervous system was finally going to end. Feeling both cautious and curious, I opened my eyes, hoping to get my bearings. I'll confess: I was disappointed to find that I was still in my room *(No bilocation? Drats!),* and I was still on my bed *(Not even levitating? Double drats!)*

Then just when I thought it was going to be among the more "ordinary" mystical experiences I'd had—well, umm, how should I put this? The only way I can think of is to just tell it like it happened:

Quite literally, above me, "a portal from heaven opened and a light shone down upon me, and the voice of the Lord spake unto me saying, 'Will you write for me? Will you be a voice for me?'"

Gosh, it was like an epiphany right out the Bible. As I mused about this event later, I could just hear the skeptics' taunts: "Oh puh-leeeze. How *predictable.* Don't you think in the last few thousand years the Almighty could have come up with some new means of revelation? A light shining down from a portal in heaven? Bite me! At least think of something original. I bet your next experience will be a burning bush..."

Honestly, I have no explanation to give to these hypothetical skeptics. Nothing. Nada. Zip. It seems they make a pretty good point. Why didn't God come in some uncommon way? I don't know. Maybe God thinks, "If it ain't broke, don't fix it." But, I'd had enough mystical experiences up to this point in my life, not to doubt what happened that evening. To me, it was as real as the chair I am sitting in as I type these words. You, on the other hand, are welcome to any opinion you'd like about the authenticity of this divine drop-in—or the state of my mental health.

However, the few people I have told this incident to have all had a completely different take on it: "I wish God would show up and tell me what to do."

I have responded every time, "Are you sure about that? God showed up and told me what to do (or rather, gave a very strong hint as to what I was to do) and I didn't like it one bit."

The truth is, although I like to write, I do not enjoy *being a writer* day after day after day. I find it a grueling task, and believe me, I can find a quatrenniakatillion other things to do to avoid it: cleaning out the kitty litter, clipping embarrassing nose hairs, and watching a few exciting hours on the *Weather Channel*, to name a few. And to say that I am not a big fan of public speaking is a *huge* understatement—like saying Hurricane Katrina was balmy with a few scattered showers. In seminary I used to rival a first-rate bulimic, routinely emptying the contents of my stomach right before speech class whenever it was my turn to read a few paltry sentences out loud to my peers. In the years since then, I have learned how to rein in the fluttering mammoths in my stomach whether I stand up to speak in front of a dozen or a few hundred. I have even begun to—wait for it—*treasure* the immediate rapport I feel emerge between orator and audience. On many occasions I have had the privilege of witnessing the significant healing energy that can be channeled through the human voice as well as the written word.

Nevertheless, I was still not happy that writing and speaking were the two main ingredients of God's recipe for my life. So I will divulge, even at the risk of looking a tad Jonah-esque, that after the Light from heaven spoke its requests to me, I did what any self-respecting mystic would do: I *argued* with it.

"But God, you know I don't like being a writer," I protested, feeling a strong affinity to all the prophets of yore who found little comfort in a divine call. "I want to do healing work."

Apparently, not in the least bit offended or deterred, the Divine gently repeated Her requests a second time, along with a promise: "I will bring you healing work. Will you write for me? Will you be a voice for me?"

I wasn't going to give in that easily, so I tweaked my tactic a bit and became the consummate model of rational pragmatism: "But I'm not making enough money. We need more money, and writing at home all day doesn't exactly bring it in."

"I will bring you what you need," was the next promise I received, followed by the requests being made for a biblical third time: "Will you write for me? Will you be a voice for me?"

Upon realizing the futility of fighting with fate—a lesson I should have already learned from my several year saga—I gave a deep, surrendering sigh, and said reluctantly, "Okay." Without warning, my heart's energy then leapt out of my chest desiring to merge with the Absolute Love hanging around the ceiling in my bedroom.

Alas, it was not to be—it probably would have killed off my physical existence right then and there. However, my slightly less than enthusiastic okay must have been enough of a yes, because just as quickly as the Light had appeared, it then disappeared, the portal closed, and the golden lava in my spine dissolved. So, in the end the Light won. Of course.

I must also confess, though, that it really wasn't news to me that God wanted me to write. For several months prior, I had been receiving a steady stream of words flowing into my mind, coming from, I presumed, Spirit. I had dutifully transcribed the words as they came, not really knowing what to do with them. It would take me several months after the Light made an impromptu house call to figure that out. The result is my healing meditation book, *You are Light*.

I'm wondering about you, though. Do you know what your life purpose is? Maybe you know exactly what it is, and you keep putting it off, pushing the idea out of the frontal lobes of your attention, because the thought of it is just a bit too uncomfortable to allow it to settle in the living room of your life. You might have to go back to school! You might have to marry (or divorce)! You might have to quit! You might have to move! You might have to _____ (you fill in the blank). The only remedy is to work through your reluctance, your fears, and your insecurities, and then seize the new opportunities that come your way.

Perhaps, however, you don't know your destiny. You wish you did know exactly what the Sacred One was asking of you. You feel stuck, stymied, and totally mired in self-doubt or any number of heavy feelings and thoughts that keep you from finding the light in the darkness. Take heart! You are not alone. You are working through exactly what you need to be working on right now at this moment. Trust your process. Trust the bigger picture. Your path will eventually be illuminated; the companions of joy, love, and peace might even surprise you along the way. Find humans, too, who can accompany you on your journey, be they counselors, healers, life coaches, or friends.

No matter whether you're reluctant, lost, or living out your higher purpose, ultimately every step of the way is a precious jewel in the beautiful crown that is your life. Never forget, the Beloved sees you, knows you, and loves you every moment of every day. You are forever held in arms of Light. I know. I've seen that Light. I've heard Love speak. That is why I write.

Questions for Reflection: What is Spirit gently asking of you? How are you being guided to fulfill your sacred purpose in this life?

[1]With a few minor changes, this chapter was originally published as an epilogue in my healing meditation book, *You are Light: 8 Words Reveal Your Truest Self*, London: O-Books, 2011.

The Other Side

Although during my saga the frequency of spiritual experiences I had multiplied like the dust bunnies mating under my sofa and chairs (and bed, table, desk, and, well, you get the idea), it was during a dark night of the soul I had a few years before my saga, that the mystical first revealed its veiled face to me. During this dark night of my soul—commonly known as "the stage of purgation" in mystical hagiography—my "shadow erupted into my consciousness" using Carl Jung's terminology. In my own terminology, I fondly refer to it as The Summer from Hell. For three solid months it felt like my soul vomited every single thing I had ever repressed or thought was bad. I confess: it was not pretty and in fact, was a downright horrifying experience. During that time, however, I learned to find light in the darkness and to unconditionally love and have compassionate understanding for even the darkest, most shadowy parts of my own underworld.

This purgation apparently cleaned out enough of my under and inner worlds that "the other side" could finally make contact and start showing itself to me. A noticeable uptick in synchronicities (another Jungian term) and other spiritual experiences began to occur. Still, it wasn't until this next event happened to me that it finally dawned on me: I had been initiated into the realms of Spirit.

I was a newly ordained pastor of a small, historic church outside of Princeton, New Jersey. This three hundred year old congregation could trace itself back before the founding of the country, and the first governor of the New Jersey colony of that time, appointed by the King of England, was a member of the originating church. Upon his death, the governor commissioned engraved silver chalices and platters to be made and given to the congregation. On special occasions, these treasures were brought out of the large, black, fire-proofed safe in the basement of the church for use during communion. Though the church had been in decline for, well, decades, their pride swelled whenever we used them. They were in their own dark night of the soul as a spiritual community, and even the ritual of bringing the silver up out of the basement, the church's own underworld, seemed to reenact the hope of new life and resurrection, of reclaiming the light in the darkness.

After a few weeks as their new minister, I was thrilled when some of the residents of a group home across the street from the church began attending worship. Previous to becoming pastor of this church, I had served as a chaplain for adults with disabilities—an incredibly healing time after my dark night of the soul. So suddenly having the group home members attend felt like a good omen to me—the least of these were honoring us with their presence—perhaps bringing their own unique healing gifts to this very disabled congregation. Most of the group home residents suffered from mental illnesses and though able to work and partly care for themselves, they still needed assistance, as living alone was not possible. One of these neighbors was a young man named David. He was a regular attendee and several of us at the church decided he would be our honorary greeter because he was so hospitable to churchgoers and guests alike.

One night, David, who occasionally told me, "I have problems," managed to take his life. It was difficult news to receive as a fledgling minister. In the same phone call that informed me of this sad news, the group home manager asked me to conduct his memorial service. I was deeply moved by this request because David held a special place in my heart—he was the first person to ever call me "pastor."

On the day of the memorial service, I arrived at the church early to prepare. Standing at the pulpit, I was looking down, leafing through my notes on the sermon I was going to give. The topic was God's compassion for all and I was using the scripture, "nothing can separate us from the love of God." I had been taught growing up that people who committed suicide were not assured of their place in heaven. I didn't believe such a thing anymore and hadn't for a long time. However, I knew there could be several people attending who might have been taught something similar, and I wanted to offer a different perspective. To my thinking, God understood David better than anyone else did. Surely, God knew all about the illness that would drive David to desperately seek his own death and escape his mental pain. And, of course, God had compassion for David's struggles and knew intimately of David's kind and welcoming heart. However, I wasn't confident my message would have much of an impact considering the grief and confusion surrounding this death, but it was all I could come up with to say.

As I was continuing to look over my sermon notes, I heard one of the old wooden swing doors in the back of the church creak, which they always did when someone opened one of them, and then I heard an old, wooden pew in the back—on the same side of the sanctuary as the creaking door—crack, which they always did as well when someone sat down in one of them. So, I casually looked up from my notes to see who had come in and sat down.

There, on the same spot of the same pew he always sat in every Sunday, was David. He was looking at me with a large, genuine smile, and I realized later this could not have been a memory, because I had never before seen him with even a hint of a smile on his face. His body was translucent, filled with light, and I knew, soul-deep and without a doubt, that he was healed and at peace. As I met his eyes, the whole sanctuary filled with a joy that lifted my eyes heavenward, and then an energy coursed through my body telling me "all is well." It lasted for just a few moments and when I returned my gaze to David's pew, he was gone.

It is the only time I have ever seen someone in full body form on "the other side" with my physical eyes. It was also the easiest memorial service I have ever had to conduct, despite the grim circumstances of David's death. A church member told me afterward, in utter shock, that it was the most joyful memorial service she had ever been to and she thanked me for talking about God's compassion for David. I never told her why there was so much joy in that sanctuary that day, nor why I could preach with such conviction that I knew David was in God's eternal arms of Love and Light. At the time, I didn't know if she or anyone would believe my story, and it was several more years before I took the risk of telling someone about it. Now I know the truth is always safe to share if I am following my inner guidance and speaking from Love, and so I offer this story here in the hope that it might bring some comfort to those grieving the loss of loved ones, especially from suicide.

No matter what dark nights our loved ones or we may encounter, there is a deeper Truth. The Love that birthed both day and night holds us eternally in the womb of God. The void is not empty—it is ever pregnant, always present, continually creating unlimited possibilities for healing and growth. No matter how dark your days, there is light. No matter how much death surrounds you, there is new life. No matter what, you are held in those strong eternal arms of Love and Light. The spirit of phoenix fire calls to you of rebirth, of resurrection, of rising out of ashes. This is always true.

May the Divine Mama bring you and your loved ones all the peace your hearts and souls need in this moment.

Questions for Reflection: When have you lived through a dark time you didn't know if you could get through? How did you make it? Do you know someone who chose to end their life? How can you honor them in your own life? What encounters have you had with someone on the other side? What blessings did it bring?

The Mowing Miracle

I confess: I'm afraid to try to start my lawn mower again. Maybe I used up all my miracle miles with it today and next weekend, the thing won't work at all.

Here's the back-story...

We've had this wonderful eco lawn mower for nine years: a rechargeable battery-operated Black and Decker that's super quiet and hasn't had any mechanical problems since we bought it. For the past two years, the battery has clearly been fading as it began to take more than the normal one recharge to mow the entire lawn. Toward the end of last year, it was taking about four charges total, two each for the front and the back to get the job done. A few months ago, when we mowed for the first time this year, it took about eight recharges to mow the entire lawn. Every week it got worse so that two weeks ago, we couldn't mow for more than about two minutes and the battery would die. We were mowing the lawn every day it didn't rain and couldn't get the whole lawn mowed over that two weeks time—by a long shot. Plus, the lawn looked terribly haphazard: The grass (and the dandelions) were at varying heights every few feet, making it look like someone very drunk, very anarchic—or both—had mowed it.

Another item of importance to this story: Our financial situation is not optimal right now. We're swamped with medical debt from my husband's ruptured disc last December. He's essentially been laid off from his position, as we haven't had a full paycheck in many weeks. We've been living on company credit cards, and more recently on personal ones. We're both applying for jobs day in and day out. Somehow I'm not really stressed about this. I know God is watching out for us. One day when I was out doing errands, I had this deep abiding peace come over me. I reflected to myself, *I know we're in God's hands, I know everything is going to turn out okay.* I then "over-heard" my spirit guides say to each other, "By golly, she's got it, she's really got it!" Right after my oh-so-hilarious guides humored themselves at my expense, I crested the top of a hill in my car and overhead I saw three eagles circling over me. I *love* confirmation from the universe: snarky disembodied voices, eagles, whatever. I'll take anything. I'm not picky.

But peaceful feelings aside, with the financial situation we're in, we can't afford to get another lawnmower, new or used, let alone a new battery. We tried using our weed-whacker as a substitute, but that just made the lawn look like someone on crack had tried to fix the drunken anarchist's work.

So yesterday, I tried to mow a little bit again in high hopes but low expectations. The mower lasted about a minute and then I had to plug it back in again. Being that today it was not raining again, I thought, *Well, I'll try and at least even up over some of the weed-whackered areas.* But after getting the mower started, within a minute (again), the needle on the battery gauge went from F to E, the battery whined in a descending pitch like it was going to die (again), and I had only mowed a couple of measly strips.

So, I prayed. "Angels of mine: I know you're good at energy and charging things. (I was also thinking, *Heck, I know this because you've been charging and shocking my body now for years rewiring me,* but I was—unlike my guides—too polite to actually put this snarky comment in as a part of my formal request.) Could you just charge this mower for me please?"

And wouldn't you know? The battery gauge stayed at empty and actually dipped below E and didn't move from there at all. Yet I was able to keep mowing. I mowed and I mowed. I was able to finish the entire front lawn and so I thought, *Gosh I should just keep going.*

So without turning it off—because I was afraid maybe it wouldn't restart if I did—I opened the gate of the fence and set off into the jungle that is our back yard. It's thick with moss, dandelions, and clover interspersed with dense weeds of mysterious origins. Add to that the thorny blackberry shoots sprouting up all around the edges of our evergreen bush-lined fence, and you see the Herculean task my battery-challenged mower had today. Even on a good day, back when the battery was working fine, our mower would bog down in it. But hey, I was able to keep mowing the back yard, too— even the tallest grass! I was also sweating like I had run a half-marathon, which time-wise was about equivalent. I must confess: I was totally worn out before the mower was, but I wasn't going to stop. It might not start again!

About an hour into my miracle mow, my husband, a true skeptic in the philosophical sense of the word, wandered into the back yard, looked at me quizzically, and questioned, "Is that still going?"

"Yup, I prayed over it and it's still going." He rolled his eyes at me in response and went back inside the house.

After another forty-five minutes when I was almost done, he came back outside again. "It's *still* going??"

"Yup," I said laughing. (Apparently, I say "yup" and "nope" a lot when I'm mowing—my backwater hillbilly ancestral genes revealing themselves when they feel most at home—outside doing chores.)

My beloved husband started coming up with all sorts of interesting "theories" as to why the mower's battery was suddenly coming to life as if it had just been transformed into the Energizer Bunny battery. "Maybe only the gauge was broken."

"Nope, the battery was totally dying after just a minute the last couple of weeks."

"Maybe, the battery just needed a good charge."

"Nope, the mower didn't ever mow the entire lawn on one charge even when it was new.

"Maybe…"

Finally, I cut him off and said, "Honey, you're looking a miracle square in the face and refusing to see it."

He retorted, "Well start praying about my job then."

"It'll be okay. The universe is giving us a sign. Everything will all be okay."

I then stepped profoundly into the middle of doggy doo-doo.

I hadn't picked up the doodie in the back yard where the dog lives before I began mowing because that would be ridiculous, nay, impossible, to think I'd be mowing the front and back lawns on the same day, let alone on the same battery charge. I had seen a couple of piles of doggy doodie when I had started mowing in the back, but I didn't want to stop the mower and go get bags to pick it up, just in case, as I've stated, it wouldn't start again. Obviously, I was rather superstitious about this miracle. Or maybe I was just selfish, but I wanted my *entire* lawn mowed, so I wouldn't risk turning off the miracle.

Thus, the doggy doodied shoe didn't bother me in the least. I guffawed heartily at the trickster prank the universe pulled on me and kept right on mowing. I mowed everything I could think of, under the bushes, on all the sides, the extra tall grass that was creeping up on the edges of everywhere—I finally had to give up. There was nothing left to mow— absolutely nothing. I even double-checked with my husband, "Do you see anything I missed?"

"Nope. It's done." (Yups and nopes are contagious, I guess.)

So reluctantly I turned my miracle off and plugged it back in. My son came home soon afterward, the one who usually does most of the mowing, and asked his dad, "How did the lawn get mowed?"

"Mom mowed it."

"How is that possible?" my son queried, knowing full well the hopelessness of trying to mow the lawn over the past few months.

"Mom says she prayed to her angels and they kept it going. We're going to be hearing about this miracle of hers for the next ten years." My son snorted.

The most mundane of miracles happened today. That's okay. I'll take it. I'm not picky. To me it shows the Source isn't just concerned with our inner workings, but also our outer workings, even the minutiae of mowers and money, or lack thereof. But hey, I'm happy—my lawn looks fantastic.

Till next week anyway.

Questions for Reflection: What are some mundane miracles you've experienced? Do you have people in your life who scoff at miracles? What part of you is a skeptic that would like to be awed by the in-breaking of the dawn into the despairing places in your life?

Visitations:
Just Call 1-800-Shower-Psychic

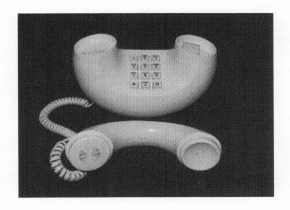

I confess: My shower stall has become the go-to-grotto for those who have passed over to the other side. Perhaps it's the energy of the water, perhaps it's the meditative sound of the water, or perhaps it's because it's one of the few places I can be totally alone and unaffected by the activity of my family—usually, anyway. Because four of us live in a small home with one tiny bathroom, even when I'm in the shower I might hear a knock-knock followed by a "Can I come in to use the bathroom?"

But usually I am isolated in that liquid vibration chamber and perhaps more receptive to picking up signals from the other side. Several people I am friends with have had loved ones pass over recently and for whatever reason their dearly departed have popped in clairvoyantly with a message right after I turn the shower on and get in. (Nudity doesn't seem to be of any great deterrent to spirits with an urgent communiqué despite my own self-consciousness at being dropped in on by total strangers while in my birthday suit.)

Mediumship isn't my calling or my specialty but it happens. However, visitations are another thing altogether. The first such visit came after the suicide of a congregant when I was a new pastor (as told in *The Other Side* above). I would not have another visitation until May 2001, when a strong, audible voice spoke out of the ethers giving me solid advice, assuring me of protection during the volatile time of my saga. From that point on, visitations have continued in my life.

On a daily basis, I experience beings making themselves known so they can do energy work and healing on me. I generally become aware of them when I see a burst of light (usually white, sometimes blue) out of my left eye. Often I see a ball of light or an orb in front of me. Other times I feel a squeeze around my abdomen and then I know some beings have connected with me, or I feel pressure somewhere on my body signaling they are trying to send some new energy into me. This pressure might take the form of the sensation of a heavy book on top of my head or of a broom handle pushing into my back at my heart chakra. Then I say what I say and do what I do to release any old energies that no longer serve my highest and best and invite in the new energies to help me shift.

During the night, my dreams are sometimes interlaced with healing experiences with beings as well. Recently I set my intention to completely heal my left hip—sore and aching from injuries in this and prior lives. I had made much progress releasing old energies, memories, and emotions, integrating new energies and fragments, yet still, even though improved, my hip pained me.

One morning after getting my teenagers off to school, I went back to my bedroom and lay down to meditate. A couple of times during the meditation I felt someone or something jump onto the end of bed, much like a cat or a young child would. I'd open my eyes to see if indeed my cat had arrived, but no, nothing was there. I wondered if it was my former cat, Marbles, paying a visit from the other side.

Soon after the second hop onto my bed, I fell into a meditative sleep and half-dreamed, half-experienced a visitation. A woman came to me—she looked just like one of the grocery clerks at a store I frequent—making me very suspicious of her whenever I shop there. *Are you a healer in disguise?* I telepathically ask her when I'm in the store. So far she's never responded at all to my attempted mind melds and goes along her clerking business as if she has no secrets to hide and can't hear me at all. Darn! She's good!

Anyway, my visitor in the dream experience stood at the end of a table I was lying on top of. She held my legs up with her arms underneath them and my left leg she held out at a more extreme angle—perhaps to accommodate the contorting twist in my left hip. She touched various points on the bottom of my hamstrings above the hollow of my inner knees.

She said telepathically, "You have too much interstitial (something I can't remember). It's causing you to have fibro-(something I can't remember, but not –myalgia). We have to remove it all and then within a couple of days we will put it back in the right amount by injecting it through your lower back."

I was awake within my dream (called lucid dreaming), and so I told her, "I'm not sure about this. Let me talk to 'Christie' (a healer friend) and consult with her first."

She nodded and added, "I need to put your body in shock now."

"Okay," I agreed.

She pushed more points under my hamstrings and my body started to vibrate and pulsate with electric shocks blasting currents through my legs and flowing through the rest of my body.

Apparently the wattage was enough to jolt my delta brain waves out of their slumbering cycles, and I completely woke up immediately after the shocks and said to the healer within my mind, *It's okay if you take it out now.*

That night I called my healer friend, Christie. She returned my call when I was out and I called her back the next morning. Before I told her anything about my healing dream visitation, I asked her what my left hip looked like.

She replied after pausing a few moments to look through her third eye to see what was being shown to her. "It looks hollow—all hollowed out. Your other hip looks full. Wait, let me look more." After a few more moments she continued, "I think it's being reborn, restored."

I then told her a little bit about my dream visitation without revealing too much. I wanted to continue to see if what she perceived matched my experience without her knowing everything that had happened. Christie pondered aloud what had been a dream, what had been my own mind's creation, and what had been real, perhaps trying to decipher fact from dream fiction. I began to tell her a few more specifics about the dream to give some concrete details, "The healer used the words interstitial something and fibro something, but that's all..."

"Wait!" Christie interrupted, "Wait—the person from your dream is talking to me! Let me hear what she's saying." She paused again and then reported that the woman told her, "You need to get the energy going by running it down Monica's leg and back and forth from hip to hip and then

Monica will be able to do it." Christie then did this which I could feel and then after I could indeed do the same things myself.

Later that day, a lot of energy started coming in through my head and my lower back—just as was predicted by my healing dream visitor. The energy influx was firehose strong and lasted several hours; the intense pressure from it required me to lie down for most of the rest of the day. The next morning, I re-consulted with Christie and asked her again what she saw. I had not previously told Christie about this part of the dream—that the dream healer had said, "Within a couple of days we will put it back in the right amount by injecting it through your lower back." So without this foreknowledge, Christie looked and said, "Your hip looks more solid—about thirty percent full and the rest is being rebuilt."

That day my hip started to feel different and better. It was a bit wobbly and I couldn't walk very well at first but in a day or two the percentage had gone up to about sixty percent, according to Christie, and soon everything about my hip felt much better. I also found I had deep integration work to do after all the energy came in leading to more soul and physical healing.

My hip joint to this day is perfect. My S-I joint is another issue altogether. Why I would receive a visit to heal my hip but not my S-I joint right along with it is beyond me. In fact, the rhyme and reason for the principles the other side operates from baffle me at times. Shower visitations from spirits? Dial-up healings for one part of my body but requests for healing the other part go unanswered? I know the rhyme and reason is there and will be revealed in time but in the meantime, I sit and wonder about what looks purely illogical and inconsistent to me, knowing that in the questions I will find the answers (eventually, anyway).

Questions for Reflection: When have you had a surprise intervention in your life? What dial-up-prayers are you sending, waiting for answers that have yet to be revealed? If you did receive an answer, what would you hope it would be? What would be even better than that?

Blinded by White

On Christmas morning 2008, we drove to my parents' home, our two-hour drive back-dropped with an occasional flurry. The ground was already white from several days' worth of cold and snow, not a very common occurrence in the Pacific Northwest. When we arrived at the street my parents live on, we stopped to assess the going forward. The only thing that stood between us and their house was a quarter mile of unplowed, twelve-inch deep, pure white powder. A giant Santa sleigh seemed a much more appropriate vehicle for helping us finish the distance and arrive bearing gifts for the noel.

Although perfectly sledless, we were nevertheless unconcerned about getting stuck because we were driving our rugged 4x4. However, another unforeseen complication arose. As we commenced to traverse the virgin snow, my husband and I realized we couldn't see anything. The snow was blaringly white, and with no tire tracks or embankments to guide us, we were essentially blind. To focus on the snowy road ahead was to become increasingly disoriented. This spatial disorientation is what happens to pilots when their airplanes are caught in a cloud, fog, or snowstorm and their instruments aren't working—they lose all sense of direction, even up or down. In order to navigate my way through, I had to look far ahead to the horizon where skyline and snowline met and just steer the car the best I could down what peripherally looked like the middle of the power poles on either side. The worst that could've happened to us was driving into a snow-filled ditch. Not fun, but not disastrous. Regardless, I confess, it was unnerving trying to drive blind with my eyes wide open.

Afterward, contemplating what it meant, I wondered what it is about white that makes everything disappear. I know white light contains all light and when refracted produces the rainbow. Is this the hidden impulse behind creation or manifestation? That the Light, the Source, is ever manifesting into varied forms in order to defeat the unknowing light, to quell the dulling blindness of sameness? By diversifying, does the Source literally come to see itself and know itself?

Questions for Reflection: What do you think is the purpose of creation or manifestation? What color is the most healing, uplifting color for you? Find a way to make sure that color is in your life today and gaze on it with an open heart. This spectral vibration has meaning for you. What do you believe it is?

The Ecstatic Factor

I'm beginning to realize that living in the energy of ecstatic bliss could be just a tad bit inconvenient to my current life. Oh dear.

I mean, I have teenagers for chrissakes. Could their mom get any weirder?

For sure, my teens have had enough experiences of their own to verify that what I talk about and live is "real." When we're in our home, our car, or anywhere private, they divulge their own little "secrets" to let me know they understand and share in my own paradigm. In public, though, it's an entirely different story. They'll take two steps back if they feel a full-on mystic mom story about to commence. If that story happens to include anything extrasensory, they are quick to disappear entirely. And by no means are they bilocating or translocating or anything else like it. They're just outta there. Gone. Split. Sayonara.

Not that I blame them. I envy them. I often wish I could disappear when the woo-woo stuff kicks in, and inconveniently, there are onlookers. Now that ecstatic bliss is emerging as an everyday reality, I confess, I'm terrified. What if I start having *When Harry Met Sally* lunchtime "outbursts" in the middle of the grocery store? What if when I'm out walking the dog, I begin spontaneously twirling like a Whirling Dervish for everyone in my neighborhood to see? What if I start laying my hands on water, and tree, on animal and bird and they heal? What if? What if? What if?

Generally, though, the fears I've had about transforming into something altogether worthy of being branded a social pariah have not materialized into reality. Thus far I've been able to merge my larger reality into my daily one. It can get a bit dicey, however. When you can see angels popping into view around people who don't believe in that sort of thing, when you can behold the absolute dazzling beauty that exists at the core of everyone no matter what they look or act like on the outside, when you can savor the autumnal colors of leaves with so much focus it feels like sucking pure joy straight through a straw into your soul, it baffles me sometimes to know how to hold both the splendor and the mundane together in the same container—the container I call my brain. How can people not believe? How can they not see? How can they not know?

I want to yell it from the rooftops. I want to laser blast them with Divine Love from my hand. I want to embrace them and never let go until they, too, know what I know.

Ooops, my ecstasy is showing again.

This bliss just gets away from me. It blows up containers of control. It blasts through walls of hatred and prejudice and judgment. It explodes the old wine skins, to quote a scripture. It's powerful stuff and I know if I go into it and live it with all my being, my own structured life might just be dynamited into smithereens. Again.

My angst about handling the increasing degree of ecstasy in my life bumped up to a new level the other day—just below DEFCON 1—(imminent nuclear threat). A pain living out in the basement of my unconscious decided to climb up the staircase and make itself known. It was a deep pain, an unresolved pain I've been carrying around since childhood, maybe longer. It felt like lifetimes of pain really. Once it appeared in the living room of my consciousness and introduced itself to me, I acknowledged it. This pain then put a DVD on in the TV screen of my mind, replaying to me visually all of the ways it had been felt in my life and in my soul.

This was the pain of "not being totally wanted." For sure, my parents wanted me, but I was too much in some ways. This was also the pain of "not being totally wanted" by my peers growing up. I was too much in too many ways. And so, this same theme has played itself out with group after group and community after community. It wasn't "rejection" because I was in fact wanted—in part. But the pain was in the partialness. It is, I suppose, just a variation of not experiencing total love by anyone in this life or perhaps for many lives except by God. I had accepted conditional love as simply part of human limitations long ago but apparently it had a twin pain I hadn't recognized at the time. Not only not totally loved, but not totally wanted.

When the DVD was done playing and I now knew this pain's story, I could say, "Thank you for showing me this. I had not realized you were living downstairs. I did hear you bumping around, but I did not know your name. Thank you for revealing yourself."

I then began affirming the true reality: that God totally wants all of me, that I totally want all the parts of me. Then the ecstatic bliss kicked in—with a whammy. Deep surges of vibrations, pulsations, and near convulsions frolicked through my body over and over. If anyone had been watching me at the time (thank Goddess no one was) it probably would've looked dreadful, like I was having a full-on, grand mal seizure. But quite the contrary, it was pleassss-ur-a-ble—far beyond anything sexual. However, this episode really had me fretting how much capacity for nuclear joy my body could carry around 24/7 without exploding uncontrollably in public places—something like having pure bliss, near-death, out-of-body experiences fully *within* your body at any time without warning. (I once met a man who had a near death bliss experience and came back with healing gifts. His body gave off so much visible light, he looked like a human light bulb!)

Barring a near death experience, it takes time and inner work to get to this place of ecstatic bliss for good reason. Some of these experiences are so intense they can fry a nervous system in a second that hasn't yet adjusted to these energies. But taking the time and doing the inner work—looking squarely in the eye at those hidden places of pain with compassionate understanding—is so worth it, reaping far more joy in the end than the temporary suffering. So much so, in fact, I've decided these ecstatic moments are worth even the risk of an occasional public humiliation. Thus, onward I march into the unknown joy. I'm willing to bet you'd risk the same to experience that bliss. Even a few moments of mindfulness a day—focusing all of your attention totally on whatever is in front of you—can start you on your way to feeling good forever. And isn't that the very definition of heaven?

Questions for Reflection: When have you felt the joy of Oneness? What happens when you practice mindfulness? What's keeping you from practicing it more?

Part Three
~Of Marriage and Children~

I Love Lucy

My husband is a tubist and during my saga before our finances took a tumble into the abyss, he bought a brand new tuba, bigger than the small antique tuba he had previously owned. A little bit of background: Many years ago I bought him a tuba stand so that he could display his antique tuba in our home. (I confess: I am proud to say I have learned the fine art of decorating with tubas.) So, I thought when he got this new bigger tuba, we would display that in the stand as well. But my hubby had told me: "No, Monica, don't put the new tuba in the stand. It's not right for it."

Well, a short time later, he went on a business trip to New Jersey and while he was away, I really thought he must be wrong. That new tuba would look really nice displayed in our sunroom. And so I put it in the stand and thought, *Wow, this does work and looks really great. I was right after all!*

The next morning, I saw that the tuba was a bit askew in the stand so I went and moved it. As I was moving it, I looked down and what to my two wretched eyes did appear, but two huge dents in the small of the bell; two dents from moving it in the stand—the stand I was not supposed to have put it into in the first place.

So I decided to try to fix the dents. I don't know why, but I thought maybe I could. Maybe I could restore the tuba so my beloved wouldn't find out and everything would be fine. Back to normal. Good as new. So I went to the kitchen, picked out a large metal serving spoon that looked perfect for the job and then went back to the tuba to repair it. It seemed the best way might be to put the big spoon down the hollow of the bell and try to pop out the dents from the inside of the bell. I did thus and started banging away on those dents with that spoon. But all that happened was I created a lot of clanging and a bunch of little bumps in the big dents making the tuba look like it had contracted a case of the metal measles.

So after that I decided to try to smooth out the big dents with the little bumps in it by running the big spoon up and down the inside of the bell and pressing the backside of the spoon firmly against the tuba. It was working a little bit except that I then noticed my efforts seemed to turn the tuba metal into rainbow colors where I had rubbed it with the metal of the spoon.

My next thought was, *Well, if I could get closer to the inside of the problem, I would be able to have a more desired effect.* So I went and found a little screwdriver to help me take the top of the tuba bell off as I had noticed there were two tiny screws helping to keep it in place. I successfully got one little screw off, but when I tried to get the other screw off I discovered it was stripped. And the more I tried to unscrew it, the more stripped it became. So realizing that this wasn't going to work either, I went to put the other screw back in and did. However, just as I was finishing tightening the first screw back into place, the head of the screw broke completely off, leaving absolutely no way to get it out again other than drilling it out. Fortunately I still had a smidgen of common sense left not to try that.

I then called my life partner, confessed my sin…s, and asked him what tuba shop I should take it to. His immediate response was, "No! Don't touch it! Wait until I get home."

So I put the tuba back in its case in the basement where I wouldn't be reminded of my sin…s and waited until he got home several days later. When he was back, it took him a couple of weeks before he was brave enough to look at what I had done. When he did, I asked him, "Can it be returned?"

His reply? "No!"

In fact, he said if I had just left it alone after the two big dents were in it, all they would have had to do to fix it was to roll a big metal ball down the bell and it would have popped them out. But now it was not repairable, replaceable, or returnable.

I confess: There was no mystical experience that made the tuba all better. All I got out of it was another Edith Bunker or *I Love Lucy* story, confirming yet again my Stupid Fool archetype.

What do you do when you've broken something beyond repair? Or your life is broken seemingly beyond repair? I have been there—when all seems lost, everything is out of your control, and restoration looks like a pipe dream at best. But it is precisely at these times that the best magic, the deeper magic as C.S. Lewis calls it, kicks into gear. The phoenix—consumed by the flame—is now free to rise from the ashes anew.

One of my professors at seminary told us this story. During his own graduate schooling, he had rented out a room from an elderly woman whom he adored. She was quite well off and had a number of beautiful things in her home. On one occasion while she was away, he was responsible for keeping up the house. Quite by accident as he was dusting, he knocked over a treasured antique vase made by a very famous artist, and it shattered. There had been only three of these that existed in the world, each worth about $60,000 at the time, and this was forty years ago.

The professor-to-be tried to repair it with glue but the cracks were still visible and anyway its value had been destroyed. He was a poor graduate student, could not repay his landlady, could not fix it, and could not buy her a new one. Even if he had the money, there weren't any available to purchase. He felt terrible and the ease with which she accepted his sincerest apology upon her return only made him feel worse.

Well, unbeknownst to him, the elderly woman happened to have a friend who knew the artist. The artist was by then elderly himself and living nearby. And this elderly woman's friend called the artist and explained to him what had happened. Wouldn't you know, that artist made the landlady another vase, for free—a one-of-a-kind—more valuable than the first.

When all is lost, somewhere there is a deeper magic waiting to be birthed. The Artiste Nonpareil is still at play behind the scenes, creating and recreating greater things than we can ever imagine or even hope for.

And now for the conclusion to the irreparable, *I Love Lucy* tuba...

We were resigned that the best we could do was try to trade it in—at a much-reduced price—for another new tuba. It took a while but finally my husband was able to find a store on the east coast that would take the damaged tuba and apply it toward the cost of a new one. However, the great Trickster was at work behind the scenes and got the last laugh. After my husband sent the tuba off on its way, we got a phone call a few days later from the shipping company. Somehow the boxed, padded, and crated instrument was totally crushed during shipping. They had no explanation for how it had happened. In the end, the shipper's insurance paid for its entire worth, as if it were brand new and had never been dented or damaged in the first place, and thus, we recovered all of our original costs. The new tuba my husband purchased with the replacement money? He was even happier with it than the one I had dented.

All was well. Again.

Questions for Reflection: When has something been so broken in your life that you despaired? How did the phoenix arise out of the ashes for you in unimaginable ways? If you are in the midst of the brokenness now, and the phoenix has not yet arisen for you, how are you being led and guided right now in the midst of the brokenness?

On Raising Intuitive Children

"Mom, what's that turquoise on your forehead?" my daughter (eight years old at the time) queried one evening when she was snuggling with me before bedtime.

I began rubbing my forehead absentmindedly, trying to get the turquoise off, thinking I must have somehow smudged myself with one of her colored markers or paint, when my daughter then screamed, "Your eyes! Your eyes! They're really, really big!"

Descending into wails of tears, she pointed at me with a revolted look on her face as if she had just seen the most ghoulish, blood-drippingly, ugly ogre ever dreamed up by a B-grade horror flick. Now, honestly, I confess I am no

Hollywood hottie even on the best of days, but I don't think I'm really all that bad looking either. So, I knew my daughter's reaction was something other than a commentary on my appearance. What her reaction was though, stymied me. I didn't know what was causing this torrent of fear about how I looked. It took quite awhile to settle her down. By then my brain had finally kicked in and I was able to put two and two together and offer her a reasoned explanation.

I had been at a healer training that day and there was a lot of energy flowing in the room we were in. By the end of the training, my "third eye" had opened for a few minutes and I had seen a swami walk into view and tell me telepathically: "You will come to see me sometime."

To which I responded to him as well as I could telepathically, "Okay, although I have no idea who you are." Then the thought popped into my mind that perhaps that didn't matter because he obviously knew who I was…

Anyway, by the time I arrived home after the training, my third eye had closed but apparently, the energy flowing in my sixth chakra (forehead energy center) was still very strong— strong enough to be seen by my daughter as "turquoise" and "really, really big eyes."

So, I told her, "Honey, it's only energy from my class today. You're seeing the color of the energy and the energy is showing you big eyes because there's so much energy flowing through my eyes, it's making them look larger than they are."

"Really?" she questioned, mopping up some tears with her pajama shirt.

"Really," I replied as confidently as I could. "That's all it is. Nothing's wrong. You're just seeing energy. My eyes are normal."

She looked hard at my eyes again, wincing in anticipation of another frightful sight, but it didn't happen. "Mom, can I fall asleep in your bed tonight?"

"Yes, that's fine. I know that was scary but there's nothing to be afraid of," and I held her in my arms until she fell asleep.

What do you do when your children exhibit "gifts" that our society does not recognize and therefore cannot support or appreciate? At the time I was still a fledgling mystic and although I was glad the explanation I offered to my daughter made enough sense to her to settle her down into sleep, I wasn't as confident in the explanation I had given as I had tried to appear.

Although this was the first time my daughter had ever remarked about seeing an aura, it certainly wasn't the first time either of my children had experienced phenomena the general public for the most part does not understand and often mislabels as "fantasy." Nor would it be the last. Over the years, they've seen energy, angels, and guides, experienced and given energy healings, had past life experiences including xenoglossy—the ability to spontaneously speak fluently in a foreign language, and exhibited intuitive soul knowledge far beyond what I was aware of as a kid. Unfortunately, a large part of society is downright hostile to anything seemingly unscientific, preferring to box anything mystical up in the wrapping "medieval gobbledygook" tied up with a bow of "loony" on top.

On the other hand, the rising tide of spiritual experiences and the outgrowth of coverage of such events in mass and social media have created pockets in society where one can go for support and help. Medical psychotherapists do past-life regressions, hospital nurses and hospice chaplains are trained in energy healing touch classes, medical doctors foray into naturopathic and other alternative modalities, police detectives use psychics and mediums for their investigations, and more.

What I have found since this aura-seeing episode by my daughter is that really all my children want is a simple reasoned explanation for what it is they occasionally see, feel, and experience. Most of the time I can give them that and they seem satisfied to put their experiences aside and continue on being a kid. By not making a big deal about what they see, they can integrate the event as within the range of normal and not get hung up about it. I often tell them, though, that a lot of kids wouldn't understand what they see and so it's good to check with me first before telling one of their friends about it. Now as teenagers they have found a few friends they can confide in when they need to and this helps them know they are not the only ones.

There have been some times, however, when I didn't know exactly what my kids were experiencing and I've needed to check in with other healers or mystics. It has been important to me to give my children the information they need so as not to create more fear of the unknown. Over the years I have put together my own network of healers, care providers, and mystics who can fill in the gaps in areas where I'm learning, too.

How do you do that? Here are my recommendations for finding more information to help yourself or your children:

1) Find an alternative health directory in your area or Google a search for alternative healers.

2) Go to alternative bookstores and ask for recommendations for local practitioners.

3) Check out books on the subject you're wondering about and look in the Resources section at the back of this book for other books, resources, and people to contact.

4) Ask trusted friends and call interfaith or unity spiritual leaders who generally are more open to the mystical and confide in them.

There are a lot of resources available out there. And hey, don't get discouraged! Just last night I watched one of Oprah's Master Classes with Martha Beck on the web and

Martha demonstrated energy testing and Oprah talked about strengthening one's aura!

Mysticism: It's the new norm. That's my mothering motto and I'm sticking to it!

Questions for Reflection: When have your children or the children in your life exhibited intuitive abilities? How is this similar to or different from your experience as a child? What can you do to encourage intuition in children? How can you help them keep this in balance with the rest of their lives?

The Year of the Hawk

When we make a choice in our life, part of this choice is done consciously in full awareness of what we are choosing and why, and part of this choice is done unconsciously, without full or even any awareness as to why we made this choice. The unconscious part of this choice is from shadow: the motivations that drive us to do things that we are not yet aware of. This unconscious shadow may come from ancestral, genetic, karmic, parental, or other hidden patterns. For example, Adult Children of Alcoholics (ACOAs) may repeatedly get into relationships with alcoholics, addicts, or irresponsible people. They may "try" not to but they continue to repeat the pattern not realizing sometimes until quite far into the development of a relationship that the person they thought they knew turns out to be a closet drinker. When ACOAs finally begin to examine their family system, perhaps looking back generations, and courageously own their own enabling, their unconsciously learned co-dependent behavior is likely to heal.

I've done quite a bit of shadow work in my life. However, I decided a couple of winters ago that it was time to start looking again at the unconscious part of some agreements in my life situations from an energetic point of view, and at a deeper level than I'd investigated the shadow previously. As I did this, I released old contracts that no longer served my highest and best as they came to my awareness, so that I could move into new, more whole and balanced contracts. After doing so during a meditation session one evening, the next morning my husband—many miles across the country on a business trip—experienced a ruptured disc in his back. This took our entire family into a new definition of crazy. He was stuck in tremendous pain in his hotel room for eleven days until he was able to manage sitting in a wheelchair so that he could get to the airport and board an airplane to Seattle—just in time for Christmas. When he arrived home, we went to the dark side as my husband's massive dosages of pain medications made him just a wee bit psychotic and slightly inappropriate. Fun!

On Christmas Day, my husband decided to stay home since venturing anywhere beyond a mile in the car could turn excruciating for him. So the kids and I drove up to my birthland a couple hours north of Seattle to spend part of the day with extended family. It really got to be humorous when the tenth hawk flew by the car windshield on the drive up. But after we had feasted and festivated we started the drive back home, only to encounter nine more hawks flying over and around the car. It was astounding. What did hawks have to do with me? I confess to having more of a blue jay animal totem with an occasional eagle thrown in for good pleasure. Hawks? Not so much.

So seeing nineteen of them within less than three hours certainly got my attention. I looked up "hawk" in my animal medicine book when I got home and found that hawks are messengers bringing divine, big picture perspective during difficult times. They are also messengers reminding us to stay in our power. A good message when pain, medicine-induced psychosis, and disability have flooded your life! Every day after Christmas Day, for about the next three months, I saw at least one hawk every day. I stopped seeing them after my dad gave me a push-pin brooch—it was a hawk! Now that I have it with me every day, I still see them, but less frequently.

It was a poignant reminder of how important it is to take a step back from the immediate crisis, no matter how pressing and imperative it seems, in order to regain perspective. I needed to hold fast to faith while also looking for the lessons to be learned amidst the crisis. A couple of days after Christmas I was able to snatch a rare walk during my husband's convalescence. As I started off, a crow flew right over me, cawed, and I felt energy come down from the crow and enter through the top of my head (crown chakra). I confess, though, that I reached up with my right hand and touched the top of my head just to make sure it hadn't become the site of some inconveniently placed crow guano. But relief! It had only been energy after all!

After my walk I went home and looked up crow medicine. Sure enough, crow medicine was about *not* poking around in the unconscious too much, or all hell will break loose. (Whoops! Sorry, hubby! Didn't mean to trigger your back blowing out by snooping around in the shadowy underworld of our relationship. Love ya! -Me.)

Crows, too, seem to be playing a more prominent role in my life. During the graveside service for my grandfather a few years back, I noticed a crow following us as we walked from the funeral hall to the cemetery where his body would be buried. As we congregated at the specific site, the crow landed high in the leafless tree right behind our gathering. At one point during the graveside ceremony, the crow started cawing incessantly. I finally realized that my grandfather was trying to get our attention to tell us he was not really "dead." During my mystical re-education that accompanied my saga, I had read that birds are often messengers for the deceased because they are easy for Spirit to use, according to Native American traditions. Why this is, I don't know, but as soon as I realized my grandpa Lester had been getting the crow to follow and caw at us, I said in my mind to the crow, "Hi Grandpa! I know it's you!" The crow stopped cawing immediately and didn't caw again.

Even in my dreamtime I have been experiencing birds, especially crows, flying very close to me from all points of the horizon. In my waketime I have been experiencing the same thing as I walk or drive in my car. My dreamtime and my waketime are eerily similar, as if there is no difference. One may simply be a reflection of the other. The dreams may represent my daily reality. Or my daily reality may be a fulfillment of foreseeing the future in my dreams. It doesn't feel like that though. The dreams don't really seem like dreams. They seem like dreamy waking times. And when birds fly so close to me when I'm walking, it doesn't seem "solid" or "real" either, more like I'm daydreaming or imagining the birds surrounding me.

It has caused me to reflect. What if my dreamtime and waketime begin to merge more and more? What will happen? What if my conscious and my unconscious were to completely merge? Is this the same process? I confess: I have no idea. I only know that birds are leading the way, teaching me to bring the unconscious to light gently, oh so gently.

Questions for Reflection: What unusual experiences have you had with birds? What contracts (written or unwritten) do you have with your partner or with other individuals or groups? What parts of those contracts no longer serve your highest and best? Are you ready to release them gently to the Light? If so, go ahead and say this out loud and then invite new contracts to come to you that do serve your highest and best. What shifts might occur? Ask that they come to you gently with everyone's highest and best in mind.

Caveman Spirituality:
Warning—Beliefs Subject to Change at Anytime without Prior Notice

I change my beliefs more often than some people change their underwear. It's not that I'm flaky, per se, though the title "The Rev. Monica McFlake" has been tossed around. Okay, I confess, I'm the one who's tossed this moniker around. You caught me. But I have been through a great many paradigm shifts. Some people stay in the same paradigm their whole lives. It baffles me how this is even possible, but I have seen that said people can grow and learn within their paradigm without necessarily shifting into a larger paradigm. Everyone's path is unique. However, when you begin to allow Spirit to lead you no matter what, Spirit may take you outside of your comfort zones.

Actually, make that *will* take you outside of your comfort zones. If you are doing your inner work, owning your shadow, and have the ability to check your own lack of integrity, you can be led to not only leave your comfort zones, you can be led right out the front door of your own sanctuaries, be they churches, synagogues, mosques, or any other religious or spiritual system. This generally requires throwing out beliefs that no longer serve your highest and best (or anyone else's either). I have found with every shift, every healing, every new energy, a few more dozen beliefs go flying out the window of my high-speed energy train. Bottom line: Don't believe everything you think. Tomorrow you may learn you have to throw out your skepticism of past lives, aura readers, energy healing, or so-called heresies, or throw out deeply ingrained teachings about scriptures, the church, the guru, good and evil, or heaven and hell. I know. At one point I heard God asking me, "Do you want me or Christianity?" Considering my church saga, I didn't hesitate, "I want you, God. And straight on till morning."

Many people inquire about how my marriage could have survived that much tectonic shaking and shifting of my internal world. My husband and I joke that his path is more along the lines of *Caveman Spirituality—Just the Basics, Ma'am.* This is our secret. We joke. A lot. At me, at him, at all the weird and wonderful things that go on in our lives. We hold very little so serious that it can't be leveled with a good dose of humor—the more tongue-in-cheek, the better.

Just today, I bought my husband his favorite trail mix. As usual on the drive home from the grocery store, I enjoyed ferreting out and wolfing down all the dark chocolate-covered almonds. When I got home and handed the invaded bag to my spouse, he eyed it suspiciously and announced: "You castrated my trail mix again, didn't you?" I laughed. He sighed. The end. (I trust you do not need me to explain his joke to you, right?)

My personal secret to marriage happiness, though, is simply to focus on myself—not selfishly—but on changing myself and no other. Rarely does this lead to confrontation, though sometimes it does. But by simply defining myself and keeping communication lines open, and working on continuing to change myself to become in better alignment with my Truest Self, my life partner then becomes my greatest mirror and teacher. By the time this goes to print, we'll have celebrated twenty-four years of marriage. Caveman spirituality or not, I'm the lucky one to have a found a man who has ridden the tsunamic waves of change in our lives and remains my best friend.

Questions for Reflection: What beliefs have you had to let go of to follow Spirit? What improbable beliefs have you had to embrace to follow Spirit? Who is likely to come along with you for the ride? Who might not?

The Baby with the Buddha Eyes

Simpatico

As above so below.
Rippled ridges of clouds formed by waves of wind
mirror the ripples in sand in the receding waves of the blue ocean's tide.
Stunted, moss-covered tree limbs high up in the Hoh Rain Forest
mimic the antlers of a herd of elk gathering in the ever-mist there—
just as stunted and mossy as the tree limbs overhead.
A murmuration of starlings—millenaries swirling in great loops in the air,
changing speed and direction in unison faster than I blink my eye,
echoes a school of fish submerged in the density of water beneath
swimming totally in synch.
The glacial blue clouds layered in the icy winter sky
reflect their earthen twins—the snowy, alpine peaks in relief below.
Everything is mirrored.
You, me.
All the parts in each part
like Mozart hearing an entire symphony in the playing of a single note.

Washington is the only state in the United States with eight climate zones, including two snowy, alpine mountain ranges, deserts, rain forests, an ocean coast, steppes, islands, and a temperate marine corridor hosting large cities, coastal towns, and rural farms. On a road trip to explore more of our beautiful, varied environment, our family ventured out to the Olympic Peninsula, visiting there a lush, torrential rain forest, and the rugged Pacific Ocean coast at La Push—made famous by the *Twilight* series. As we stood on the sand dunes at First Beach, the wind blasting a sea chill through our bones and my cells feeling like the wind was going to blow them away as easily as it did the grains of sand at our feet, we gazed in wonder at the rock formations jutting up out of the water like giant ocean stalagmites. Out of the corner of my eye, I spied a baby with big brown eyes in the arms of his mother nearby. Although it was Labor Day weekend, and technically still summer, we were thoroughly refrigerated in a matter of minutes and so we turned around to hike back to the parking lot a few hundred feet away.

As I did, I looked at that adorable child, deep into those big baby browns with my full awareness. In an instant, we—the infant and I—were locked in the gaze of Oneness. His awareness was huge—his old soul was even larger and when the connection, the recognition occurred, a throaty giggle gurgled up from his belly. He laughed and laughed far more than a mere baby. It was an eternal soul's delight at being thus perceived. Nay, it was The Soul laughing at his/herself in the Universal Mirror, at the simpatico everywhere and in everyone. Buddha eyes. A Buddha laugh. A buddhaha moment.

His parents were clearly delighted by their gregarious baby, seemingly unaware of the rapport that had occurred between him and me. For how could a baby have such a Buddha or Christ awareness as an infant? No matter how difficult to believe, I confess I know it's possible. Daskalos, a famous Christian mystic healer from Cyprus, interviewed in the O magazine before he passed over, was deeply aware as a child: he could perform healings, speak fluently in the languages of his past lives, and could give specific details of his past lives that could be historically validated. As a young child, his marvels were well documented, though often considered suspect due to local superstitious beliefs at that time. People I know myself, too, report seeing and knowing things as infants that seem incredulous on face value.

Sai Baba, a well-known Hindu miracle worker, was one such of these. I have no known connection to him, but a client of mine does. As my client was on the healing table, I led her into an exercise to facilitate a decision process. When her heart opened, as did her emotions, she connected to Sai Baba—still living in body at the time. I then felt a strong burst of energy come down and around me, like a powerful energy showerhead had suddenly turned on above my head. I *knew* Sai had given me a blessing.

Blessings come from anyone and everyone, even baby Buddhas. They come from anywhere, from Sai Baba in India, and from God in heaven, which is everywhere. Blessings abound. The universe has our back and is ready to shower us with energy, even laughter if we have the eyes to see, the ears to hear, the mind to wonder, and the heart open. When we align our inner world with the paradigm of blessing, then it is not simply "as above so below," but also "as within so without." "For what you achieve inwardly will change outer reality."[1]

Questions for Reflection: When have you looked and seen an old soul in a baby's eyes? What internal blessings do you want to birth to be mirrored back by the simpatico soul of the world?

---

[1] Otto Rank, psychotherapist contemporary of Carl Jung

The Secret to a Bliss-Filled Holiday

"Every child comes with a message that God is not yet discouraged."

~Rabindranath Tagore

Advent, Kwanzaa, Hanukkah, Winter Solstice, and Christmas. Holidays. *Holy*-days. They mark the time, heralding that a sacred season is upon us again.

But does not every turn of the earth as it spins around old Sol signify the unshakable faithfulness of the Beloved? Is not every moment imbued with the holy?

Indeed. Yet, daily chores and routines can so easily lull us into a spiritual hibernation. We forget who we are and why we are here and we sleep through our so-called waking hours. Thus in collective wisdom, special days and seasons have been set aside to help us wake back up to Reality.

Every season is sacred.

Every day is holy.

Every moment is extraordinary.

Remembering this throughout the year takes a great deal of practice and a lot of mindfulness. I calculated the possibilities. If every moment that we stay in the "now" lasts about a second, there are 86,400 "nows" in every day, and more than 31 million "nows" in every year! I confess it's no wonder to me now, why I so often fall off the "stay in the present moment" bandwagon.

But during this tumultuous time of deep change in the world and the accompanying surface uncertainties, it is even more important to strive to live in this continual state of awareness. Doing so may require even more effort on our parts, but living in the ever-present moment reaps its own hearty rewards. Have you ever experienced a high from gazing intently at the vibrant, red hues of a poinsettia flower? Or the incredible bliss from saturating yourself in the flavor of the orange juice you are drinking?

This is just a taste of the paradise available every moment of every day. All it takes is focus. Concentrate on an experience with all of your attention and with one or more or all of your senses. When you totally focus on an event, or a person, place, or thing, you become one with it in the moment. This is sacred Oneness—the root of all joy—and the key to staying awake to Reality. I set the intention during the winter holidays that every time I see a twinkling of light, whether by candle fire, electric fire power, or star fire, I will reawaken to the now and to who I am. Mindfulness is one of the best roads to take on the way home to bliss, whether on a "holy-day" or an "ordinary day."

But there is yet another stanza in the carol I am singing this year.

Every season is holy.

Every day is divine.

Every moment is magical…and…

During the Christian holiday season, the expectation and birth of the Christ child are celebrated. In one scriptural story, Anna, a prophetess, and Simeon, a man guided by Spirit, see the infant Jesus in the temple when Mary and Joseph have brought him there for the first time. Anna begins praising God and Simeon declares, "Here he is, the one we have been waiting for…a light…this child is destined…"

One person has asked, "What if Anna and Simeon were led by Spirit to praise God and announce these words with every new child's first appearance at the temple?"

Hmm. Interesting question.

When I was very pregnant with my daughter and my son was nearing three years old, we traveled back to our homeland of Seattle for the 1995 holidays—not on a donkey, thank God, but via the airways from New Jersey. (Now that I think about it, I'm not sure how much better that flight was than a donkey ride. For five long hours, my husband, my toddler, and my pregnant self, were stuck on a plane in the throes of a spectacularly virulent stomach virus we had all contracted just before getting on board. Ugly doesn't begin to describe it. The only holy moment I can recall during that inflight flu fête was when I realized I no longer feared, as I usually did, plummeting to earth in a fiery plume. In fact, I confess, I desired it.)

Anyway, on Christmas Eve that year we attended a play in Seattle that depicted the traditional nativity story with a modern twist. The angels, the shepherds, the wise men, and even Herod appeared in their scenes to each sing a popular Disney song or show tune with the words adapted for the scene. For example, when the wise men appeared, they started singing, "Oh, We Just Can't Wait to See the King," sung to one of the tunes from *The Lion King* movie. Likewise when Herod appeared, he began singing, "I Did It My Way." It was quite clever and humorous and my son, an avid soaker-upper of all things Disney, was entranced.

A few weeks later, back in New Jersey, my daughter was born and within a couple of days we were sent home from the hospital happy and well. One afternoon soon afterward, my son snuggled close to me while I was resting on our living room sofa. He looked up at me with a furrowed brow of concerned contemplation and asked me quizzically, "Mommy, when are the wise men going to come to our house?"

In his enlightened sensibility, informed by the Christmas Eve play, the wise men were supposed to arrive after every new baby's birth. What if that did happen in our world? What if wise women and men announced the birth of every child as divine promise and arrived soon afterward, bestowing each new soul born with gifts and symbols of the spiritual presence inherent within? What if this were a holiday ritual for all children to help them remember who they are? Would our world heal?

For is not every child sacred? Is not every baby a divine spark made manifest? Does not every birth herald the promise of renewed Holy presence and purpose among us? Is not every infant another face of God?

Every season is sacred.

Every night is divine.

Every moment is miraculous.

Every child is holy.

Look into an infant's eyes this season and see the light of the Beloved shining through them. Be a wise woman or man and offer spiritual gifts and words of blessing to little children and grown-ups, too, who have yet to meet the Divine Child within. And let the twinkling of lights in the night reawaken you to the now and remind you who you are.

Blissful Holidays to one and all!

Questions for Reflection: How will you celebrate the sacredness of a holy season in a new way this year? How can you celebrate the Child Within throughout the year?

Part Four
~Of Animals and Nature~

The Dancing Universe

It happened again. A dog just went a little cuckoo when he saw me. I was in line inside the local bank waiting my turn to make a rare non-ATM transaction. A man who was being attended to by one of the tellers had a non-seeing-eye dog with him. (We're very dog friendly in our neighborhood—in fact, Seattle boasts more dogs than children.) As the man finished and turned to leave, his dog saw me, immediately came over to me, and then started spinning rapidly in circles at my feet. In the middle of the lobby. If he had been a little Chihuahua, maybe no one would have noticed. But alas, he was a rather large dog and so, one-by-one, I saw heads pop up, turn, and glance in my general direction. You couldn't *not*

notice the dog's bizarre behavior. Even the dog's owner was looking at me like, *What the heck??*

I thought to myself, *Awk-ward. Make this end, Monica. Now!* Who knows? Maybe I have a little lingering past life anxiety from witch-hunts and didn't want the locals observing the magic I live with every day. Regardless, after realizing the potential implications of having my community see too much, I quickly acted by warmly greeting the dog with my hand, sending love energy through it to him, which made him stop his dizzying circles so he could lick me to his delight. Then the owner called him and his dog left following behind him, reluctantly I presumed, as the dog kept turning his head and looking back at me.

It's important to mention that I had come to the bank directly after giving someone a healing session. So my energy was flowing well and apparently the dog in the bank lobby agreed. "Hey this feels *good*! Let's play in this energy for awhile!" It wouldn't have looked any weirder if the dog had stood up on his hind legs and started dancing a jig with me.

I confess: it isn't the first time by any means. I have had three dogs, completely unfamiliar to me, come up to me and lie down on my feet. Not at my feet. *On* my feet. One dog in particular was a very high-strung dog. It was another occasion where I had just done a healing session with someone. I was sitting in a chair in the home of a friend who has a frenetic, high-strung dog. (I often imagine this dog's thoughts are akin to, "Ohmigod. Ohmigod. Oh. My. God! Everything's terrible! Doom's around the corner! All is lost! Ohmigod. Ohmigod. Oh. My. God!" But I may be projecting.)

Anyway, this large, neurotic canine came over and lay down across my feet and stayed there until I left. The dog's owner remarked, "Wow, she likes you. She never stays still for strangers." Another dog that did the same was a greasy, junkyard dog, and my son's friend's dog has as well. I have also witnessed a dog pull its leash away from the person walking her, pick up the leash in her mouth, and then carry it over to me.

Hey, what can I say? Dogs like me! But I confess, it's not really me. It's healing energy. They *love* it. They thrive in it. In fact, all of nature responds immediately and spontaneously when any of us are vibrating in the energy of love and joy. My miracle cat, Marbles, would spin rapidly in circles at the feet of a healer friend of mine whenever he did a healing with one of us in our home. Then she'd twist and torque her body much like the doggy in the photo, not stopping until the healing session had concluded. The universe is alive and dancing. We are the dance and the dancer. Won't you join in?

P.S. Since this event occurred, for sacred activism reasons, I have happily switched back to banking at a credit union. Power to the people!

Questions for Reflection: What experiences have you had with nature or animals that reflect this divine truth? When you are in the company of a person or animal who loves you unconditionally, how does your body feel? Give yourself that feeling right now and let your body dance!

Meditate Like an Otter

Growing up in the Pacific Northwest, some of my fondest memories are of deep-sea fishing on the North Puget Sound with my family. We spent many hours of many weekends bobbing around the straits surrounding Vancouver Island in our little motorboat, occasionally reeling in huge king salmon that weighed upward of 35 pounds—half of my body weight when in I was in elementary school.

For those of you not in the know, the Puget Sound (or Salish Sea, as the indigenous people call it) is a meandering body of salt water connecting the Pacific Ocean to the inner port cities of Washington State; cities that are otherwise separated from the Ocean by the vast Olympic Peninsula.

Teeming with marine life, spotted with rustic islands, framed by alp-like mountains to the north, west, and east, the Sound is full of visual treasures that dived deep into my soul as a child. Riding on its often glassy surface was like being mounted on a liquid horse whose gait was smooth, sure, and as unforced as a cloud floating on air.

Whenever I have been away from the area, I have never felt fully back home until I have stood on the shores of the Sound or drifted on its depth, smelling again its briny foam, and pondering the ancient mysteries of its being—the watery womb from which all life on earth was birthed.

During one of our boating expeditions, the seas took a decidedly nasty turn for the worse. It was not too rough for our boat size, but I heard my mom decry a much smaller boat than ours a distance away that looked like it was being tossed about in the choppy, white-capped waves. "How dangerous! How foolish!" she exclaimed about the two fishermen who dared to continue to brave the stormy weather.

Without saying a word my dad nonchalantly changed directions, motoring over to the smaller boat, perhaps for us to assist if necessary. When we were close enough, we could see that my mom's "small boat with the two fishermen" was in actuality a log with two seagulls standing on it. Mom had forgotten her eyeglasses on that trip.

Looking back on it, despite my intense enjoyment being on the Sound, there were times I felt as vulnerable as a flightless bird on a log in the middle of those often treacherous waters that could turn from a smooth, glassy surface to twenty-foot swells with just a shift of the wind. We nearly capsized once in just such a scenario because my dad had a big fish on the line and didn't want to give it up to find shelter amidst the squall.

Not every outing contained a barf-over-the-side-of-the-boat dramatic adventure—some were far worse. On one such occasion, we had seen a pod of Orcas sporting in the distance. Such sights weren't rare but they were infrequent enough that it was a real treat. As we continued on our way, trolling herring for bait, we entered a narrow channel situated between two small emerald isles.

Right after doing so, my dad remarked, "Look at all the fish!" We peered over the edge of the boat and saw what must have been thousands of herring right below the surface of the water, transfiguring the normally cobalt sea into fluid ribbons of silver. We had never seen such a sight. We continued being dazzled while Nature showed off her flashy side with this spontaneous sparkler show, when I heard my dad mutter something under his breath and out of the corner of my eye spied him stand up and start reeling in the fishing lines—fast. I turned to see why my dad, seaworthy through and through, looked rather peaked and was acting a little manic. My mom then screamed. Loud. For there upon our boat's stern (did I mention that our boat, though bigger than a seagull-ridden log, was not even close to yacht-sized?) was the entire pod of Orcas. My breath caught in my chest like I was the one who had been hooked by one of our fishing lines. It was awesome, terrifying, and exhilarating all at once. They began swimming by us. And I mean, *right* by us. Any one of us could have had a "reach out and touch someone" moment with an antediluvian Goliath of earth's primordial waters.

My mom's screams turned to yells: "Get us out of here! Now!" she ordered my dad.

"If we make a sudden movement, the whales will act to protect their young," my dad replied evenly. "They're keeping their young on the outer edges of the pod, away from us. If we steer suddenly they won't like it. We need to stay where we are. They see us, and they'll go around us. Stay calm." Truly, my dad was assessing the situation with more measured wisdom than my mom, but even with only eight years of life under my belt, I was old enough to detect a tenor of tense falsetto in his voice, all the same.

Regardless, it was impossible to make any kind of a move. Where could we go? They surrounded us on all sides, and we were in the middle of a narrow channel, tucked in by two close islands.

Protective of her own young, my mom continued screaming to the high heavens. She was having none of my father's cool-headed rationale, disguised well or not, and as an eight-year-old following her mother's cues, I confess, neither was I. It was only when a great Leviathan surfaced right beside our boat, revealing a large intelligent eye that gazed directly at us, that my mom was finally stunned into silence. She spent the remaining minutes, as the pod slowly made its way past us, hiccupping the suppressed sobbing that happens when you know the deep is going to break over you any second and the only prevention is total containment.

After all those black and white mammals—the pandas of the sea—did make their way by us and through the narrow channel, they started up their sport again: frolicking and leaping into the surf, spouting, and generally having a grand ol' time. Without the perceived threat of being overturned with three small children on board, our family could then take delight in the play of these beautiful, behemoth ballerinas and realize how blessed we had been by their presence—despite the sheer terror of those eternally-lasting few minutes.

I was reminded of these epic voyages this past summer while accompanying my daughter to swim lessons. She decided she was finally going to overcome her fear of water, and so I spent many mornings of several weeks at a chlorine-atmosphered indoor pool, excitedly anticipating her success. And indeed, she became a competent, confident deep-end swimmer by the summer's end. I'll confess, though: it surely wasn't the imitation aquamarine water in the pool that created the mental transport to my sea-nurtured childhood. The agent of my flashback was a brown-haired, pixie-like, pre-school girl.

She was probably about four-years old and day after day she, too, showed up for swim lessons. She was quite an adept swimmer for one so young. The problem was she couldn't swim "properly," that is, in a straight line, with head in the water, taking side breaths, and kicking her legs without bending her knees. Week after week, the instructors would patiently show her the "proper" way to swim, and week after week, she would just keep swimming her own way without passing her classes.

Her mother was often mortified, offering an exasperated sigh every time her daughter bobbed up and down, and swam spinning and weaving across the pool. The little cherub wasn't obstinate or afraid. Far from it. She was fearlessly giving it her all. But her young limbs and nimble body didn't understand "straight."

One morning in particular, the contemplative in me caught hold again of this little girl's plight. As I watched and pondered, in an instant I was back in our little boat on the rollicking waves of the Puget Sound's straits as my dad was heading us in the direction of an island shore to investigate some curious splashes he had eagle-eyed. As we approached, I pointed and shouted with glee, "Otters!" We all admired their brown fur glistening like stars in the sparkling waters as they came close to us, diving and rolling, wrestling and playing, turning, and jumping—never stopping and never swimming "straight."

Here was the answer: The little girl in the pool embodied an otter in an artificial aquarium habitat; her olive skin and brown hair hearkening to their sleek amber fur, as well as her continual rolling over, swimming this way and that, up and down, never a fear, just buoyant delight. After realizing this girl was channeling a sea creature, I leaned over to her mom and said, "You know, your daughter reminds me of an otter."

She sat motionless for a moment and then nodded vigorously, "Yes, that's it!"

I never saw the little otter girl after that week. I don't know if the mom suddenly appreciated the epiphany that her daughter already was a proficient swimmer and gave up classes for the time being, or whether her schedule changed. Regardless, upon reflecting on this scene I couldn't help but realize the irony, if not downright absurdity, of trying to train an otter how to swim "properly."

But isn't that what we do to our souls when we try to follow "shoulds" rather than joy? Our truest selves are innately playful, naturally buoyant in the realms of Spirit just like otters and Orcas. Never fearing, our souls leap and frolic and roll around, purely delighting in the deep sea of being. But we straightjacket our souls every time we try to meditate "the right way," or spend years pursuing the "proper career" while our heart withers, or whenever we tell ourselves joy isn't natural.

Why do we try to train our souls away from their innate wisdom?

The answer eludes me, but I've learned over time to pick up the signals when I'm sliding back into the ruts and routines of monotony. For example, when I catch myself saying, "I *should* meditate," I double-check to see if I'm forcing my soul into something that doesn't fit right at the moment. I've learned to ask, "What *does* my soul want right now?" Instead of my usual meditation, maybe my soul wants to take a contemplative walk, or a nap, read some inspirational poems, or dance nekked in the moonlight. And no, I have never done the nekked dance thing. Ever. Enough! Stop asking about it!

Our souls need space and freedom. Some people mediate better visually, some actively with their bodies, some through music or dance (nekked or clothed), chanting or painting. In other words, do what comes naturally to your soul, listen to what it loves. And remember, forcing your soul to meditate a certain way or even work according to prescribed rules makes about as much sense as teaching an otter how to swim properly.

The seas of my childhood are now within my soul, continually beckoning me to come out and frolic in the play of being. Today I play with words.

Questions for Reflection: Where are you being invited for some soul play today?

Modern Day Dr. Doolittles:
Myth or Unfathomed Mystery?

"If we could talk to the animals, just imagine it…
What a lovely place the world would be…
If we could walk with the animals, talk with the animals…
That's a big step forward you'll agree…"

~song lyrics from the *Dr. Doolittle* film, 1967

Not long ago, a coyote was trapped in an elevator in downtown Seattle. The Sarvey Wildlife Center was called and they sent out a staff member who calmly talked the coyote into a crate without using any force or a tranquilizer.[1] A coyote whisperer?

Stories like these are on the rise and Hollywood has joined the foray with the current popular television show, *The Dog Whisperer*, as well as the film of a few years back, *The Horse Whisperer*. In alternative health directories, one can find an assorted number of people who call themselves "animal communicators" and advertise themselves as specializing in telepathic communication with pets and wildlife.

Does this show we are experiencing some significant leap forward in consciousness on the planet?

According to religious myth, Adam and Eve at first had the ability to converse freely with animals and were at ease with all of Nature. After "the Fall" occurred, humanity lost this paradisiacal relationship. In many literary myths, this innocence lost is portrayed as never having been broken in the first place. For example, in *The Lion, the Witch and the Wardrobe*, by C.S. Lewis, when the four Pevensie children are magically transported to the land of Narnia, a beaver meets them to give them advice and guide them to safety.

Peter, the eldest tells the others, "I think we should listen to the beaver."

Susan, the logical and sensible one, contests, "It's a *beaver*. It shouldn't be saying *anything*."

As the children continue their journey, they are surprised to find that animals, birds, and even trees can speak their language, and that it has always been this way in Narnia.

What if our own ability to communicate with animals has never really been lost? What if we just are becoming aware (again?) that this is possible? What if the logical, sensible parts of ourselves that tell us that this is impossible are, well, just plain wrong? I confess: I'm more than willing to believe this is true.

Last year for the first time, my mom went to the home of a friend who had recently lost her husband. This friend has a talking bird—an African Grey Parrot named George. My mom reported that he was incredibly verbal with an extensive vocabulary. As my mom and her friend talked, George chattered away seemingly in his own world, when suddenly he said, "Time for her to go!" (apparently referring to my mom).

My mom's friend replied automatically, as if having a discussion with a bird was perfectly normal, "No, she's going to stay longer and talk for awhile." This seemed to satisfy George who didn't mention it again.

At one point as my mom and her friend continued their conversation, my mom noticed it getting darker outside and thus, inside as well. My mom thought to herself, *It's getting dark in here. She needs to turn on the lights.*

Without a second's delay, George piped up, "Turn on the lights! Turn on the lights! It's dark in here!"

Coincidence? Or some type of human and animal telepathy? Either way, it unnerved my mom to no end. "That bird read my mind!" she often says about the experience. George went on to make comments and say other unusual things that evening about his owner's deceased husband that seemed to suggest George knew exactly what was going on.

It would be human arrogance to think that the potential for human-animal communication is only so that we can help heal animals. Animals themselves may help us heal and have a lot to do with helping the planet heal as well. Last night I dreamt of horses—horses that could speak. In the dream, they were talking to me in English, but no one else could hear them. They spoke of harmony and balance between masculinity and femininity and between intimacy and individuality. These horses were human whisperers, pointing me in the direction of my own continued healing.

I recently read a news article that told the story of three lions in Ethiopia who chased off a twelve-year-old girl's abductors and stood guard around her for half a day until the police and her family found her. Upon seeing the girl's rescuers approaching, the Triune Lions simply retreated into the forest behind them. Perhaps all our animal sisters and brothers are human whisperers—whisperers guiding us into a renewal of our Edenic beginnings, reminding us of our own humanity.

The thing is: to hear a whisper you have to be listening.

Questions for Reflection: Reflect back on your own life, especially your childhood. Have you had any experiences with animal-human communication? What does the possibility for animal-human communication mean for your daily life? For the planet?

[1] Another story from the Sarvey Wildlife Center about an amazing eagle named Freedom is a case in point. The wildlife center rehabbed this dying eagle and now she in turn is helping to heal others.

Go to www.sarveywildlife.org/Story.aspx?id=7 for this inspirational story.

Doggy Divine

Usually, among we esoteric types, we speak of the God-Within, referring to the divine essence or "spark" that is at the core of each of our beings. This "God-Within" is our Truest Self, having within itSelf all of the eternal qualities of beingness: light, love, joy, abundance, truth, freedom, peace, and wisdom in unlimited supply.

This "God-Within" awareness is activated uniquely in each person. Some awaken to their Truest Selves gradually over much time, perhaps even lifetimes. Some awaken suddenly with a momentous blast of insight and they spend the rest of their lives working out the implications to match their new understanding. Some awaken through a life devoted to service, devotion, or Nature. Each path is unique, as is each moment of awakening.

For many, the path to awakening comes through self-love. This self-love is not selfish pride or excessive egoism. This self-love is simply an application of the Divine unconditional love and infinite regard applied to the individuated self. It is an attitude of appreciation for your life, the gifts given, for all aspects of your unique, personal incarnation of eternal Love and Beingness. It is knowing this Love for the self—feeling it, thinking it, acting on it, caring for it. Of course, all is held in balance. Self-love is not indulgence or putting one's own value above another's value. Care and love of the self is shared with others equally because everyone is an expression of the eternal One Self. When we truly love ourselves in entirety without condition, it is then possible to love the other, even the enemy.

However, for many people, there is no connection in their life to unconditional Love. There is no person who has demonstrated unconditional regard and infinite Love for them, so they think they don't have love and have a hard time connecting to it, even when it's right in front of them. Having never had a divine experience of it in their life they don't know what it feels like and so if you tell the person, "Feel love for yourself. Respect yourself. Appreciate you," you're likely to get a blank stare or a confused look.

This is exactly what I got back when I suggested this to a client. "What does that look like?" the client asked me when I said that loving herself would help her heal. When I talked about feeling good about herself and taking care of herself, all of that sort of self-help lingo thing, she still looked back at me like I was speaking an untranslatable foreign language. Nothing. Nada. Zip. No connection. No idea whatsoever what I was talking about.

Then, I confess, I blurted out, knowing in a split second it was the right thing to say to her, "Think of yourself as a dog."

She looked at me as if I'd just Tasered her, and then we both started laughing.

I mean, how absurd to tell someone who was struggling with her self-image, "Think of yourself as a dog." Yeah, that'll help. Sure, Monica.

But it worked. Why? Because she had told me previously that her only real experience with love—both giving and receiving it—was with dogs. It was her only connection, but it was a strong one.

So, in suggesting she think of herself as a dog, it helped get her mind around the complete block she had as to how to go about thinking about, feeling, and acting on loving herself.

"Oh!" she said, "That's good. I didn't think you'd be able to get past that block, especially so fast, but you did. I can do this. I get it. I do."

And then I had her close her eyes and imagine the Dog-Within and how she would love this dog. She has since reported that practicing this has helped her when she is with someone who makes her feel judged about herself. She goes to the Dog-Within and comforts it and speaks soothingly to it. This settles her down and she is able to interact without the unease of condemning thoughts and feelings about herself coming from the other person, real or imagined.

Dogs and pets in general can be a powerful connection to Divine Love. Because animals do not judge, the essence in them that is Divine comes through with no mental or emotional hang-ups—just straight up Love. If you are having a hard time connecting with self-love, just imagine your inner self as your favorite pet or animal, and send and receive Love from that place. You'll begin to get a taste of the wonderful flavor of unconditional Love for you.

Questions for Reflection: What pets or other animals have you known that connected you to Divine Love? What does loving yourself mean to you? How can you express that self-love today to yourself and to others?

The Trees Speak

"Stones have been known to move and trees to speak."
Macbeth
~Shakespeare

My favorite Dr. Seuss book as a child was *The Lorax*. In the story, a greedy entrepreneur begins indiscriminately cutting down the plentiful fluffy fruity trees native to the town. The entrepreneur sees only profits in the colorful tufted trees whose tufts he can transform into a unitard called a "thneed"—with the marketing tagline "something everyone needs." The Lorax, a strange Seussian character, pops up one day to defend the Truffula trees with his famous line: "I speak for the trees for the trees have no tongues." The Lorax repeatedly protests the decimation of their forest for pollution inducing profit. This proves to be prophetic for in time, the town becomes a deserted, toxic, industrial wasteland. The only hope given in the end is one seed preserved from the now-extinct trees and the word "unless." A poignant word: unless…

Unless we hear the trees speak, what will become of our world?

I confess: I have heard trees speak.

One morning, I had an especially difficult, nay, impossible time getting out of bed. This happens on occasion when my subconscious hasn't finished processing the integration that was happening in a dream. Most of these times when I try to wake up but instead remain in some form of a half-sleep/half-trance state, something significant happens: a healing, an information download, or an energy transfer.

However, this morning none of these were occurring, yet I still couldn't wake up. I'd start to get out of bed and then would quite literally fall back on my bed and into a fitful sleep. This happened repeatedly over a two-hour period from about seven to nine in the morning. There was no fighting it. The dreams were bizarre. I was bleeding out of the top of my head and babies—many babies—were flowing out of my head. I was trying to save my babies but there were too many and I couldn't stop the birthing process.

When two hours later I finally could get up and stay awake successfully, I followed my typical morning routine prepping for the day, and then walked out of my house to get in the car to run some errands. I was stunned to see that there was a tree company working in our neighborhood and they had chopped off the top half of one of the evergreen trees in our front yard. Another evergreen in a neighboring yard had the top third of it chopped off. The tree workers were hired to "trim" the trees around the electricity wires in our town. I wasn't surprised to see that the workers all sported military-style buzz cuts. Apparently, trim = butch in their vocabulary.

Was this then the source of my dreams and my perpetual dream state? Was I so connected to the energy of the trees around me that I could sense their pain, their "bleeding," and their intention to save and multiply themselves through birthing cones? Were the trees talking to me? I have no other explanation.

A minister friend of mine was walking to work one morning as he normally did. On his route, he would pass by a large, beautiful oak he loved and admired. That particular morning he felt the impulse to bless the tree and stopped and laid his hands on it. He silently began to bless the tree, when clear as a bell he heard these strong words in his head, "*You* don't need to bless *me*. Let *me* bless *you*.*" Immediately, he felt a surge of bright intense energy from head to toe.

I, too, have had an ecstatic moment with a tree. A vibrant red maple in the backyard of our former house filled up the view through the paned windows of our sunroom. I was lying on a sofa there in open-eyed meditation and the tree grabbed my attention. I started to do a visual contemplative exercise focusing totally on the tree's rich ruby leaves. After a few moments, I became one with it and experienced so much bliss I thought my body might explode like Vesuvius on steroids. It felt, I confess, orgasmic. Dr. Judith Orloff, an intuitive psychologist and professor at UCLA, tells of a similar experience while meditating with a tree.

Trees are great and powerful beings with a story to tell and energetic gifts to share. They play a crucial role in the interconnected order of all things. Most trees if not cut down will outlive a human life by many generations. Oddly, soon after writing this, one of my neighbors decided to hack off a large part of a tree in the front corner of my yard. He is not my next-door neighbor so the tree was not protruding onto his property. He just decided he didn't like its proximity to the road, so he hacked off over seventy-five percent of it without permission. Putting aside the inconsiderate nature of his action, let alone the illegality of it as far as our city's policies go, it grieved me. I could feel the shock of the tree and I still don't know if it will survive the trauma. Such callous disregard for the life of a tree! I feel like the Lorax in me is rising and I may have to echo another clergywoman's practice of holding a memorial service for every tree cut down in her neighborhood to honor its life and life-giving.

Our worldview that sees non-humans as expendable must change. Everything has consciousness. Everything. It doesn't mean then that trees can never be cut down or plants and even animals not eaten. But when you realize that everything is energy and that consciousness on some level pervades all, you become more aware of the cost of cutting down a tree. There is a circulation of energy that happens between everything that exists—material and non-material, sentient and inert. Most westerners consume without conscious awareness and respect. Hugging, or better yet, meditating or praying with trees, can put us in touch with the fact that trees, do in fact, have tongues, and do communicate on their own level. The question is: What are they saying?

Questions for Reflection: What trees have been important in your life? Take the time to visit the tree and say thank you to it. Visualize the tree if visiting is not possible. I also recommend reading the poem, *The Sycamore,* by Wendell Berry.

Metamorphing Bears

A while ago a brown bear had been spotted roaming through Seattle's wooded neighborhoods. Authorities determined the young male bear probably took a wrong turn and instead of heading into the mountains, went right into the city. Soon afterward, it showed up on the sports track of my daughter's middle school before most students and teachers had arrived for the day. Nevertheless, it created quite a stir in our community. We received several formal notifications all day long from the school and the school district via robo-phone calls and robo-emails telling us that students had been advised to stay away from the bear. (Litigation Prevention 101.)

These alerts contained a lot of unintentional humor in giving out "helpful" information as far as what to do and what not to do if anyone encountered the bear.

"The Department of Fish and Wildlife advises that if you see a bear: Remain calm. If it approaches you, stand up, act like a human, and wave your hands above your head and talk in a low voice..."

Act like a human? What do people normally do when they see a bear? Act like an animal? An insect? A bird? And exactly how is waving your hands above your head and talking in a low voice, "acting like a human"? If everyone I know went around acting like that I think I'd start to believe in a zombie apocalypse after all.

"Don't run unless safety is near and you are certain you can reach it. Climbing a tree generally is not recommended..."

Climbing a tree generally is not recommended? What the exceptions are to this general rule, I want to know. Is it only trees that aren't recommended? Can you climb something else? Are there any times when climbing a tree would be recommended—like say when you notice the bear has its arm in a sling?

"Don't use the word 'bear' because it might associate the word with food. People feeding bears often say 'here bear'..."

People are known to feed wild bears by saying, "Here bear, here bear"? If I ever meet anyone who has ever done this, I would like to sell them some land—prime, fertile, unsullied, and at the bottom of the Pacific.

Apparently, wildlife officials have seen the gamut of what people will do, climb, or say, around wildlife, and thus, the need for those oh-so-obvious warnings that abound nowadays, even on small appliances, such as, "Do not use this toaster for heating liquid." The warnings from Fish and Wildlife concluded:

"If the bear comes after you, clap your hands and yell. Use pepper spray if you have it."

This reminds me of the joke about the hiker getting ready to travel into grizzly bear country. He buys a bear bell and attaches it to his pack, adds a pepper spray can to his outside pocket, then attends the ranger's lecture on recognizing grizzlies: "How are they different from brown bears?" the ranger asks rhetorically. "Well, one way, of course, is to compare their scat (droppings). Y'see, grizzly scat has bells in it and smells like pepper..."

On the day of the local sightings, I wore a brown sweater, brown beaded earrings, brown shoes, and a brown purse to honor and cheer on the bear. I didn't think I'd be mistaken for the bear, as I don't weigh 250 pounds. After putting this oh-so-newsy self fashion report on Facebook, a friend posted in reply: "Actually, this bear is reportedly about 125-150 pounds. Better wear a bear-bell necklace!"

Regardless, I had no fear of the bear. I wanted to see him not avoid him, so I went driving through a forested drive north of the school (the bear was noted to be gradually moving north), hoping for a lucky break to encounter him from safely inside my car. While I was out and about I could tell I was connecting to this bear energetically. At one point, I drove around a bend and saw him. There he was right in front of me on the left side of the road next to the creek. His brown shape was unmistakable against the forested new green leaves of spring. As I drove closer, suddenly my vision changed, and the bear metamorphed into a big rock, leaving me feeling, I confess, rather crestfallen.

I found out later, the bear had been through that area merely an hour earlier than my error. However, I've had enough experiences to know not to completely dismiss my bear vision. Was I so connecting to the energy of the bear, that I could see its spirit and energy imprinted on the similarly shaped and sized rock? I've seen other items in nature (branches, trees, plants) "appear" as animals when I first glance at them, only to have them "change" back into their ordinary state a few seconds later. According to Jamie Sams, a prolific and well-known Native medicine woman, this sort of thing begins to happen as those on the spiritual path enter into the fifth and sixth initiations of the medicine wheel. The energy of the land begins appearing through its other forms.

"Some people begin to glimpse these [energetic] patterns when they...see the forms or faces in tree knots or a stone...This ability is developed when we slightly change our perception and allow the spirits of nature to bring the spark of life and the patterns within solid objects into our perceptions."[1]

The news reported later that day that because of the bear's elusiveness, those looking to catch him in order to relocate him had named him, "The Urban Phantom." Sublime!

Shape-shifting abilities abound in myth. The transfiguration of Jesus is a key part of the Christian story. Even our culture has embraced the metamorphing legend of the Quileute people who can shape-shift into wolves, as highlighted in the *Twilight* series. However, the more people there are who continue to shift into their Divine consciousness, the more shape-shifting may no longer be the stuff of ancient myth and legend. A friend once told me after we had meditated together that during the meditation, she had opened her eyes and saw my energy turn to pure light, sending pulsing vibrations through her. I didn't know it had even happened, though there were clues that pointed to the truth of it: for a few hours after the meditation all I could see was light inside my head and I had an odd kind of headache.

Even Nature may transfigure itself. On a contemplative walk, I observed a cloud that was regular in every way: white, puffy, and generally round in shape. Upon my gazing at the plain Jane cloud, it turned instantly into a giant question mark and then it shape-shifted again into the image of the all-seeing eye. I did not imagine or hallucinate this. It happened with the physicality of the cloud.

The phantom bear was on an adventure: bear dogs after it, continually eluding the best catchers, hiding out in woods by day, traveling by night, seeking its home—a safe haven in the wilds however far it had gone astray. This shape-shifting metamorph taught me yet again that all forms are phantoms: fleeting and ephemeral, here today and gone tomorrow. Only Spirit remains.

Questions for Reflection: What shape-shifting adventures have you experienced? What can you metamorph into to play out some fun adventure in your life?

[1]Sams, Jamie. *Dancing the Dream.* San Francisco: Harper, 1998, p. 236.

Part Five
~Of Movies and Pop Culture~

How Sci-Fi of You!

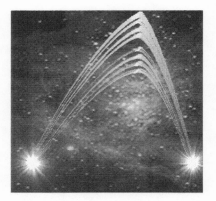

I confess: I'm a sci-fi geek. I love *Star Trek*, *Star Wars*, and all the rest. You will not, however, find me in any costume uniforms from stated series affixed with faux communication gadgets—even on Halloween. Maybe I'll save that until I'm in my "When I'm 60 I'll wear purple" stage of life. Or maybe not.

There are a lot of spiritual leaders, teachers, and healers that like to dress the part: flowy robes or exotic foreign clothes, or even clerical collars as the case may be. I only wore the collar when it was required as it did help in certain settings, such as at weddings and in hospitals. Without it, people assume the woman in a suit could not be the chaplain, the officiant, the minister. But otherwise, incognito suits me better.

However, dressing the part is a custom found in all cultures throughout human history. The one set apart for spiritual leadership is identified through the donning of various symbolic, recognizable markings. Just this morning I saw a man walking slowly (meditatively?) by his house with a sarong skirt, flip-flop sandals, and a neon pink fauxhawk, accented by the severely shaved sides of his head. He certainly looked like he was signifying himself as different, especially as this was in a suburban residential neighborhood. He didn't look dressed in any traditional religious garments that I could identify but, nonetheless, I knew he was marking himself as spiritual, as set apart, as focused on the other worlds.

For myself, I imagine incognito suits me better because it is all so *real* to me: the sci-fi and the spiritual. It blends together, and I like to participate in this blending. Watching old reruns of *Star Trek: The Next Generation,* I've observed mind melds, telekinesis, and telepathy—lots of telepathy, and healings happen by energy transfers through touch. I know people who do these on a regular basis. Okay, I confess, I *am* people who do these on a regular basis. The telepathy for me though is sporadic. If someone else is telepathic and sends me a message, I receive it. Sometimes I can hear other people's thoughts: my husband's, my children's, my clients'. I can also hear my angels' and guides' thoughts, though I usually text message with them for accuracy. Yes. Text message. Using pendulum and alphabet chart. Works fabulously.

Even before I was a mystic or even aware that I was a mystic-in-the-making, my maternal intuition was already spot-on accurate. When I was pregnant with my first-born, a son, I crocheted a blanket. Shocking, I know, especially considering I'm the anti-Martha. It's the only craft I can do and I haven't done that craft in, oh I don't know, sixteen years or so since I was pregnant with my second and last baby. All crafts stopped once I was done giving birth. I had created the ultimate, a baby. How could I compete with that? A blanket? *Come on!*

Anyway, when I was crocheting those blankets I was sure, absolutely sure, I was making a neutral-looking, androgynous-colored blanket that was appropriate for either gender, since we didn't know the sex of our babies beforehand. When I was done with my first baby-to-be's blanket, I looked at it and said, "That looks like a boy's blanket!" and sure enough we had a boy. Same thing with my second baby-to-be's blanket except I said upon completing it, "That looks like a girl's blanket!" and sure enough we had a girl. Since then I have had 100% accuracy predicting the gender of a baby-to-be. I don't have to crochet a blanket to find out anymore, though, I just use that pendulum and text message it.

When I can't text message with the universe, the telepathy can come in handy. On a trip to mid-Minnesota for a working vacation, we were traveling on a state route a bit up north. The sun had just dipped below the tree-line in that heavily forested area, dimming the sky to a smoky charcoal hue. My husband turned on the headlights in order to see better, as night would fall soon. Just before we were about to round a bend in the highway, I heard the word, "DEER!" formed very loudly and clearly in my head (red flag!). I then heard "DEER! DEER! DEER! DEER!" (Red Flag!!) repeating like an incessant alarm. It became so pronounced in my head I started saying it out loud along with whoever/whatever was telepathically communicating with me. My husband started to slow the car as he thought I had seen a deer, but I hadn't. Just then, we rounded the forested corner and standing right beside the highway's shoulder was a large herd of deer.

I've had these telepathic warning moments with other animals. I once was about to pick up an open-topped box in the garage. I heard the word "RAT" in my head, (RED FLAG!!!), right before I picked up the box but ignored the telepathic message and picked up the box anyway, to my own detriment. As I lifted the box, the weight of the box shifted and then out flew a large, brown rat right at my face. I screamed, dropped the box, went just a little berserk—shaking my head, waving my arms, and dancing my feet—like I was an honest-to-goodness Shaker-in-trance, and moved out of the way, all in the same split second. When the rat landed on the floor it ran as fast as it could out of the garage. I'm not sure who was more scared. To say I'm not a huge fan of the majority of the mammalian order, rodentia, is a huge understatement—like saying the International Space Station has a view. Now it turns out, rats show compassion for each other, sometimes more than humans show for each other. I'm not sure what to do with that information. I confess: I want to keep abhorring those plague-bearing beasts.

Anyway, what intrigues me about telepathy and the like in this day and age is that we are now technologically able to approximate these intuitive gifts with sci-fi-ish machines: mobile phones and computers provide instant communication around the globe (something telepaths and energy readers can do), Kirlian photography reveals auras (something clairvoyants can do), brain printing reveals the truth (something an energy kinesiologist can do), MRIs show disease (something a medical intuitive can do), and blood tests determine the gender of a baby (something I can do with simply a necklace) to provide just a few examples. Science is catching up to the mystical. The question is: at what cost? At what cost to humanity for the technology? And at what cost to the Mama Terra for the resources to produce such hi-tech, sci-fi-ish abilities? All of these sci-fi abilities humanity can do if it embarks on the spiritual path of integration—a more personally challenging task than the technological short-cuts that get there the easy way. And these mystical abilities are cheap and green.

Our technological advances have gotten far ahead of our wisdom and collective ethics. Perhaps it's important to mark myself as a spiritual leader after all, rather than to blend in, in order to be able to question, and even more importantly, in order to be able to call out the Divine Wisdom (the Sophia) in us all. If you catch me at my next book-signing wearing a red *Star Trek* uniform, or flowy purple robes from India, don't be too surprised.

Questions for Reflection: What sci-fi abilities do you have or are you aware of in others? What do you think about the idea that technology is a substitute for meaningful spiritual practice and gifts? How can you raise your spiritual practice to the next level?

Waiting for Godo...

The title does not contain a typo. What inspired the intentional misspelling was some reflection on the conundrum of what to call "All That Is" or what in western beliefs is traditionally referred to as "God." At Princeton Seminary, it was clear in our classes and required readings that feminist theologians were the primary movers and shakers in re-imagining our traditional lingo: Goddess, Gyd, G*d...Why not Godo?

In the play, *Waiting for Godot* (correctly pronounced GOD-o, hence the intentional misspelling of the title), two down-and-out men wait and wait for an acquaintance, named Godot, who never appears. There is much speculation about whether this play is an allegory for life—waiting for a God who never shows up to make things better. Regardless, the play is definitely a reflection on waiting, for isn't most of life waiting? As children we wait to become teenagers, then we wait until we can drive, graduate, go to college, then to start a career, then maybe to get married or have children In time, we wait to retire, and perhaps then some wait to die. (As a mom I confess I've waited and waited: until my children slept through the night, weaned themselves, were potty-trained, were old enough to go to school, then off to college, and then I'll be waiting till they're out of the nest, as bittersweet as the darkest dark chocolate as that seems to me now.)

Even on a daily basis, we wait and wait. We wait at the traffic light, in the grocery checkout line, and for our favorite TV show to come on. Or, we wait until we will have more money, or find a better job, or until we are finally healed. In Seattle, this kind of waiting is famously rendered in a sculpture of several people standing by the side of the road, as seen in the picture above. It's titled: "Waiting for the Interurban"—a reference to a promised transit line that has never materialized.

Why do we keep waiting to be satisfied? Why do we think, "When I have this thing or person or event or situation, then I will finally be happy?" Why, after waiting and waiting our entire lives, and never being fulfilled, do we keep waiting like the down-and-out characters of the play?

In the movie, *The Last Samurai*, the warrior-poet Lord Katsumoto, played brilliantly by Ken Watanabe opposite Tom Cruise, seeks to find the perfect cherry blossom—a spiritual quest. It is not until his very last breath that he realizes and speaks his final words, "They are all perfect."

He finally finds peace on his deathbed. Many do find peace on their deathbeds, but fortunately we don't have to wait to die to find this peace! As spiritual teachers everywhere have recommended, we can die before we die. How? By dying to the ego, that is, to the belief that who we are is separate and disconnected from "All That Is."

When one has awakened to the Beingness that is beyond all names and language but that exists in all, one knows that waiting for fulfillment, or perfection, or the right person, or whatever that next thing is that is going to solve everything is an empty chase, a hunger filled for a time that soon becomes ravenous again. When you become aware of Reality, you stop waiting! The moment is now. All is perfect. The satisfaction, the happiness, whatever it is you seek, is already fulfilled. It just is. Dwell in the now. There is nothing in this particular moment that you need, so enjoy it. You are well. Only the memories of the past or the pining for a potential future keep you from your happiness.

Still waiting for Godo?

Godo or "All That Is" is within you. No waiting needed anymore.

Questions for Reflection: What are you waiting for to make you feel happy? How can you give yourself this feeling right now?

Glitches in the Matrix:
The Bat, the Cat, and the Rat

In the movie, *The Matrix*, what everyone believes is the real world, is actually a computer-generated virtual reality, maintained by energy obtained from permanently incubating humans. These human batteries maintain the computer mind that runs the world via a computer program called "the matrix." In order for humans to thrive and even survive, though, they need meaning and connection. Thus, this computer-generated matrix provides a collective virtual world for all of the human minds attached to it, making them believe they inhabit busy lives, with jobs, relationships, homes, etc. This virtual human reality is completely illusory as it exists only within the computer program. Within this matrix program interactions do happen via the choices of the human incubators' minds, but free will is only allowed within the parameters of the computer program. These parameters also help the matrix to stay nearly undetectable.

However, in the plot, some people have awakened to the true reality of the world, harsh as it is, and have found a way to escape their battery-incubated enslavement as computer fuel. It then becomes their mission to rescue others while fighting off the computer trying to destroy or re-enslave them.

It is pointed out in the movie by those who have escaped the clutches of the matrix that when they have gone back into the matrix to attempt a subversive rescue and they see a glitch in the matrix (such as seeing the same black cat walking across their path twice in a row in the same direction), this is a sign the computer mind has become aware of their rebel actions within the matrix. The matrix will then intervene within its program to try to head the rebels off and attack them—much like a virus detection system. These glitches— the same thing happening twice in a row—are the clues the rebels use to know they need to hurry up, change course, or get the heck out of the virtual reality before they're caught.

Needless to say, this is a very negative view of the future of the world. Though there certainly are parallels to a mystical paradigm, the mystic sees the real world as essentially good. For this mystic, yours truly, the real Matrix (Latin for mother) is the divinely encoded universal field of energy that, left undisturbed by human minds, manifests as love, abundance, peace, joy, harmony, balance, etc. This energy womb is that from which we (and all matter) sprang and from which we shall all return.

Our Divine Mama Matrix is infinitely caring and supporting us. The rub is that the *human* generated matrix of our collective thoughts, beliefs, emotions, and actions has imposed a rather harsh, vengeful, competitive virtual reality on the world that produces greed, corruption, starvation, and violence—shielding us from seeing the essential good that is ever flowing in us, to us, and through us.

As we heal back into our original Wholeness, as we awaken to the Divine Mama Matrix, we, like the rebels, want to help others awaken, too. But we want to help people heal by realizing the false, harsh matrix is the illusion. The real Matrix is only Love. When you have realized this Love, this Divine Mama Matrix within yourself and the entire universe starts to show Herself to you. This can be a blast, because she is a Hoot!

For example, the other evening on a stroll with my husband, we approached the corner in the road next to our house. Night had just fallen as softly as a sheet descending onto a bed, though the street lamps illumined our path sufficiently to see adequately and walk safely.

As we were turning the corner by our house, I noticed a bat fly right above us. I then looked down and a cat streaked in front of us. A few more steps and I saw a rat run under a neighbor's front porch. A bat. A cat. A rat. Just like that in a matter of less than five seconds. It was so digitally timed it felt like a glitch in the matrix, comical and poetic—too Shel Silversteinish not to notice.

And on days when the Trickster energy is high, such as on the day of a full moon or the beginning of mercury going retrograde, a coyote has inevitably run out of the woods right in front of my car as I've driven down our hill's road. The coyotes have each then turned as soon as they reached the street right in front of my car, and started to run downhill in front of me. These coyotes continued to run ahead of my car for about five hundred feet—like a coyote escort—and then turned off back into the woods. This has happened a few times, all at high noon—not typically when coyotes show themselves. To me, it is the Matrix showing me a glitch to warn me to be on the lookout for unexpected twists, making me more alert and aware and, I believe, safe.

For some reason, when I traveled overseas, the Mama Matrix showed up a lot. Perhaps this was for protection, giving us synchronicities of provision and transportation exactly when we needed them, because otherwise we would have been at the mercy of the elements and without a translator to facilitate any help. Or perhaps leaving the familiar matrix of our own culture took off our illusory blinders, so to speak, making us more aware and more open to the larger Divine Matrix at work everywhere at all times. On a couple occasions when I was traveling, though, the glitches that happened were so exceedingly unexpected, I can only think again of the Mama Matrix's humor.

A group of us were living in the tribal Philippines one summer. We were there to help a local village build a community center and during the weekends we would explore the outer regions through hiking, as there were no roads or motorized transport in these remote areas. These tribes had only in recent decades stopped being cannibals, and they were still largely animists—who believed in the spirits of everything—the living, the dead, the animate, and the inanimate. This is not really all that different from my current paradigm, except that this wasn't an idealized aboriginal spirituality where all is Love. Rather, these were spirits to be feared, who demanded retribution through revenge killings on enemy tribes, and used to demand the eating of said murdered enemy. These were spirits who exacted disease as punishment, killed babies if the parents had offended the spirits, and generally stirred up a lot of suspicion and enmity. Somehow in the midst of all of this fear, though, we lived among the most hospitable, generous, and giving people I have ever met.

Anyway, on one hike, we grew in awe at the famed Ifugao rice terraces, considered by many to be one of the great wonders of the world. Their emerald water cascaded down hillside after lush hillside of steep, terraced mountains as the tropic sun amplified the jewel rich hues, mesmerizing us into a kind of lucid dream-like state. However, we snapped out of our dazzled daze as we rounded the corner of the trail and came face-to-face with a g-string-wearing, spear-carrying young man in full tribal feathered headdress. We stopped in our tracks, stunned into silence by the close proximity of a warrior in every sense of the word. Conversation was out of the question, we all knew, for in this area few people spoke English and he looked like he could speak English about as much as we all looked like we could speak Ifugao. He looked us over and then said cheerily, "Good morning!" in as perfectly authentic of an American accent as any of us could produce. He turned the corner and left, quickly hidden from our vision by the turns in the trail. We surmised wryly that he must be back home on summer break from Yale. Glitch in the matrix? You tell me!

On another such hike, we went to watch a pig sacrifice by the local shaman. He was conducting a ritual to hear from the spirits who they were to revenge kill for a murder of a woman in their tribe. The word "eerie" doesn't begin to do this ceremony justice. Pigs squealing, chanting, smoke, suspicion everywhere as the revenge dance took place high on a bluff overlooking a steep cliff. We kept our distance. Since I was studying cultural anthropology, I confess, I was curious more than I could stand, but within a few minutes of observing the scene, I felt an overwhelming sense of oppression and had a terrific headache. In a short amount of time, we all wanted to get out of there as fast as possible, and so began hiking back down the hill's trail.

We reached the main road safely and started hiking towards the village that had become our summer home, not talking much, as we were all digesting the vivid scene we had just witnessed. As we approached a bend in the road, suddenly a white van sped around the corner. How long had it been since we had seen a van? Jeepneys were all that made it up the roads this far into the hills of Luzon Island. The van seemed as foreign as we were—out of place in every way. The van screeched to a halt beside us, and a man jumped out with a large envelope in his hand. "Special delivery for John Abbott" (our team leader). John walked up, took the package, signed for it, and off sped the van driver, back down the hill. The Divine's incredible sense of timing: gut-wrenching humor even in a gut-wrenchingly dark place. We all thought this would make a fantastic commercial for Fed-Ex, though I don't think any of us followed through with submitting the idea once we had traveled around through various countries in East Asia and arrived back home in Seattle.

The Living Loving Matrix likes to play and if we're paying attention will grab our attention to show us that what appears as real is just a form of the Really Real. In this human matrix we all participate in, light and dark, joy and suffering all play a part in the drama, helping us to wake up. And as more of us do wake up, massive deconstruction of the current fear-based human matrix will begin to happen naturally. Then the Good Mamma Matrix playing poetically and humorously behind it all will be seen and merged with, so a new human matrix can be born in Love and Harmony for all.

Questions for Reflection: How do glitches in the matrix show up for you? How is the Real Matrix of Love trying to reveal itself to you? Where do you need to wake up?

Irreverent Reverence

In honor of April Fool's Day I dedicate these words to all the holy fools throughout history who have lightened society and our souls with their wise folly. In researching the origins of this day, I found they remain in obscurity—appropriately so, I think. Part of the confusion arises from the fact that some sort of "fool's day" is celebrated in many different cultures and countries around the world. Where did it all begin? Who knows? Everyone's got a different theory. I guess we're all fools when it comes to knowing anything about April Fool's Day!

What is established historically is that in western cultures the court jester often embodied wise folly. The jester was usually a marginalized person of society, who, having gained the life wisdom that comes from being rejected by the status quo, is able to see through the machinations of human and institutional ego and poke fun at it. Society and the royals freed the jester to speak truth to power without bearing the typical retaliation for doing so. (Wouldn't that be nice?) Our political cartoonists and late-night comedians embody much of this archetype today.

In my own life, I am reminded of wise folly not just on April Fool's Day, but in nature as well. In Pacific Northwest Native cultures the blue jay represents the archetypal fool or trickster, who, through its cluelessness, inadvertently brings transformation to the group. I think of this every time I hear a blue jay cackle its throaty laugh.

I have also seen wise folly through the eyes of my children, especially in the vast number of children's fables and tales that cast the fool as the hero of the story. Think of *The Emperor's New Clothes* and especially books by Dr. Seuss. On an Easter Sunday, my children and I spent the afternoon at the movies, watching the delightful Seuss classic, *Horton Hears a Who,* with marvelous voice-over work by Jim Carrey, Steve Carell, and Carol Burnett (during which my husband stayed home and napped deservedly after a very long morning playing the tuba through four Easter services.)

Horton is a perfect picture of holy folly...

even though his news
that he'll save all the Whos
sounds like a plan that was hatched
by a head full of thatch...

(and to the good Doctor - my deepest contrition
for this feeble attempt at a rhyme à la Seussian.)

The lovable Horton is willing to risk everything for the truth and *not* willing to be forced into traditional understandings of the way things are. I confess: I was a little blubbery by the end of the movie when not only is Horton vindicated, but Horton then includes those who ridiculed him in helping him accomplish his supposedly far-fetched plan. As the credits began to roll, the audience broke into appreciative applause—a rare thing at the movies these days.

Some time ago, I felt a bit of holy folly in taking a Gallup Poll over the phone. After the typical political, economic, and healthcare queries, their religious questions stumped me.

"Are you religious?"

"Yes and no," I retorted without much thought.

The Gallup pollster didn't like this one bit. (I'm sure she always colors inside the lines.)

"Are you *religious*?" she asked again, more emphatically, as if I had simply misheard her.

"What do you mean by religious?" I parried.

"It's your opinion only, ma'am."

"Umm, I don't know," I finally conceded. "Do you have any questions about spirituality?" I wondered aloud.

"No," was her terse reply.

A few questions later I was again stymied.

"Are you a Christian or non-Christian?"

"Both."

"One or the other, ma'am."

"Neither applies then."

The pollster gave a big sigh of exasperation. I was pretty darned sure if she could have reached her arm through the phone line, she would have decked me, God bless her. I wasn't *trying* to be as annoying as a rickety wheel on a shopping cart that just won't go along with things, but I couldn't pigeonhole myself into any of their traditional religious categories.

Never one to let a pollster have the last say, however, after finishing the rather lengthy survey, I went to Gallup's website and sent a comment their way. Hopefully, some en-"lighten"-ment was transferred to that traditional of pollsters—things have changed—there's a whole new world now of inter-faith and inter-spirituality. Perhaps it's time to rethink and rephrase your questions on religion?

I hope I made Horton proud.

Questions for Reflection: Who are the holy fools in your life? When have you embodied wise folly?

Truthiness in My Throat

Throat Chakra Symbol

The Miriam-Webster dictionary definition of "truthiness"…

truthiness (noun). 1: "truth that comes from the gut, not books" (Stephen Colbert, Comedy Central's *The Colbert Report*, October 2005).

Truthiness is a word from a political satire talk show intended to mock the way presidents, politicians, and political pundits do "truth." It may not have any facts or evidence behind it, but truthiness is what someone emotionally believes to be true, anyway.

I confess, though, that as an intuitive I can honestly say I get truthiness. A lot of what I believe intuitively, I am unable to verify with facts or evidence. The facts and evidence do tend to sway in my direction eventually—bearing out that my intuitive knowing is tapping into some larger pool of information that I have learned to heed regardless of appearances or apparent evidence.

I relied on trusting my gut during my several year whistle-blowing saga. It didn't let me down even once. If I had listened to the wisdom of others, or trusted what was written down or said "factually," or ignored the gut warnings and third (stomach) chakra spinnings of my larger truthiness, I would have gone down with the Titanic. Fast.

So, here's to the truthiness that prevails when the facts don't!

All satire aside, I am aware of how off much that is presented as truth in political discourse is. However, I do take issue with Colbert's definition of truthiness as "intuitive knowing" and suggest that instead, "truthiness" actually means believing in something because of self-interest, or self-investment in one's own paradigm or worldview. If a politician has devoted his or her entire career to a certain political party, and the facts and evidence show that some of the ways that party has led the country have been disastrous, rather than do some inner searching to find out why the model, the political paradigm didn't work, they just go on believing the same paradigm, trusting the same principles that created the mess in the first place. When confronted with the facts, they start spouting truthiness, ignoring the obvious elephant in the room, with passionate commitment and doomed certainty.

It would be too much work, too much soul-searching to re-evaluate one's beliefs and one's paradigm. It could be too costly, too time-consuming, and too painful. What if what I have devoted my entire life and career to turns out to be "wrong" or "too limited" or "false"? Yikes! How do you re-form your life and your career after realizing that? What do you ever believe in again? What is truth? A good question Pontius Pilate asked Jesus at his trial.

And here is where the rubber meets the road. Is there truth that "facts" and "evidence" don't support? What do we do with truth that one has to jettison in order to move into greater truth?

What I'm getting at is that there are layers and levels of truth. In this model, borrowed from Zen mystic philosopher and author Ken Wilber, truth can be seen as a great nest. This great nest contains a series of concentric circles. Each circle represents a paradigm or worldview. The smallest circle in the middle is the smallest worldview representing a very limited perspective, perhaps someone who is only interested in what benefits that person alone, what we might call narcissistic or egocentric. We're all there when we're two years old, but most of us grow out of it as we age.

As people and societies inevitably do grow and mature on the whole, their paradigms naturally enlarge through education and experience. Each larger circle or worldview represents a wider awareness of truth that is more inclusive of additional knowledge and wisdom. The larger the paradigm, the more integral one's perspective. In this concentric circle model, then, truth is always limited to one's paradigm. People who can see a larger paradigm can generally see a larger truth. What may appear to be fact and truth at one level of concentric circle is not fact or truth at a larger level.

Consider this simple metaphor. If on video you see a person punch another person in the face, you might believe this is indisputable fact and therefore truth. However, perhaps you see the same incident from another angle or a more encompassing view and you discover that it was all an act and the person only faked hitting the other person who also faked being hit. What looked like indisputable fact from a single vantage point, from a more encompassing, more inclusive vantage point, is found out to be false—not because the person holding the belief was wrong, lying, or had bad intentions, but simply because they literally could not see the larger truth.

In Wilber's model, there is truth at every level in every paradigm because Spirit is present in all. But the challenge is for us to be willing to let go of smaller truths in order to grasp larger truths. This is quite an undertaking because it can require more letting go than is comfortable, including letting go of one's spiritual or religious community, perhaps even changing spouses, careers, friends, etc. And it is not necessarily a one-time thing. We continue to evolve and grow if we are willing to continue to let go of limiting beliefs and "truths" as they are revealed and this may require letting go of more people, places, and communities we hold dear. It also involves being willing to let go of our perceptions of ourselves and ultimate reality. For religiously and politically held dogma, this can indeed be very unsettling. Simply put, it is the willingness not just to be born again, but the willingness to be born again and again and again and again—the willingness to be an eternal mother of oneself.

This is where intuitive truth can help us. Intuitive truth, while not infallible as the person receiving the intuitive knowing can still interpret what is received in a limited fashion, it still comes directly from the Source of all knowledge and wisdom. Intuitive knowing, therefore, contains within it the possibility of breaking us out of our limited paradigms and personal blind spots to seeing something more than the "facts" might show us at any given time.

Lately, I seem to have a throat that holds me to this larger truth. Whenever I speak or even read truth that is simply more limited than I know to be the bigger picture, my throat's energy begins to constrict and go catawampus. For example, a few weeks ago, I picked up a book on the display counter in the library written by none other than the esteemed (and rightly so) Dalai Lama. I opened it to a random page and began to read. It was a section on karma and as I read, my throat started to constrict extremely painfully. It was only after my throat squeezed tighter than if a boa constrictor were wrapped around it that I realized that the Dalai Lama's view of karma was very mechanistic. I embrace a more dynamic view of karma that involves grace and soul choice, not just a tit for a tat or an eye for an eye. To be sure, the energy constriction in my throat happened *before* I had any thoughts or reactions to what I was reading. My energy "spoke" before my mind! When I realized what was going on, I closed the book fast and put it back down on the display shelf. My throat started feeling better immediately. In other words, I needed to trust my own truth more than the Dalai Lama's!

It took me quite awhile to come to terms with this. I mean, how do you trust your own truth so much you have the chutzpah of an outcast woman to say to someone like Jesus when he dismisses you, "Even the dogs eat the crumbs that fall from their masters' table"? (Matthew 15:27, NRSV)

I also had another experience when I had to communicate something unpleasant for a business transaction. My neck went into a painful crick the morning before the conversation took place and didn't release until the next day when I realized I had given the person's potential response too much power over me. My neck started feeling better instantly. The truth in my throat had revealed itself yet again. I had spoken from a place of too-limited truth for me that included me giving away my feelings of confidence to someone else's control.

This truthful knowing that is beyond my own mind reveals itself as well if I say something that is even a smidgen off the whole truth to the extent that I know it. I immediately feel my throat's energy wobble or constrict. Yesterday, I went to hear my children participate in a church service. I have made it a practice since my mystical awakening, not to join in particular phrases in singing or in unison prayers that I know don't fit my paradigm anymore. During one song, which is one I normally enjoy singing due to the melody and energy, I was singing and not singing on a phrase-by-phrase basis— bizarre as it, I'm sure, sounded to the pewsitter in front of me. Nevertheless, on the last verse, I wanted to sing the whole darned stanza because the music is so majestic and singing this phrase and then not that phrase is just, well, odd. So, even though I knew that one phrase in the last stanza wasn't truth for me, I started to sing it anyway. I regretted it immediately as my throat again constricted painfully. My throat just won't let me get away with anything!

So, I propose to the god of late night political satire, Stephen Colbert (a holy fool whom I adore right along with Jon Stewart), that truthiness is truly less than truth, but it is not gut-knowing truth. Intuitive knowing, that is gut-knowing, or even throat-knowing, goes in the opposite direction of truthiness. It points to the Truth in us all, yet beyond us all. Politicians as well as spiritual leaders, teachers, and healers may say they are speaking truth from their gut, but that doesn't mean they are. I once had a spiritual healer who was typically highly accurate in her intuitive knowing tell me that if I didn't come to her class (and pay her $500), I was going to be in a car accident—which would cost me a lot more than $500. Besides the fact that my deductible was $500 so it would have been even steven either way, I knew that her personal self interest and self investment in my attendance had thrown her intuitive knowing into the level of truthiness. Needless to say, I didn't attend her class and was never in a subsequent car accident.

Your inner Self is your own best guide. Trust your gut. Your throat. Whatever. All truthiness and satire aside.

Questions for Reflection: When has your intuitive-knowing been right regardless of what others have said or advised? Women's intuition is both revered and mocked. How do you know when your own intuition or another's intuition is off and revealing "truthiness"?

Harry Potter, Anyone?

"One thought—thought well—travels ten thousand miles."

~Unknown

As I write this, *Harry Potter and the Deathly Hallows, Part Two,* is being released in theaters around the country. My son has quite literally grown up with Harry, having entered kindergarten the year the first book, *The Sorcerer's Stone,* was published, and having graduated from high school the same year as this final film. I confess: Sometimes I believe JK

Rowling is really a closet shaman who has simply concocted an "alternative reality" story based on what is in actuality her real reality to let us all in on her magic. I give in to this fantasy of mine because there are so many things in the Harry Potter world that are in fact, parallels to my own mystical reality. From defeating fear-based boggarts (household spirits that cause mischief) with laughter, to animal patroni (read: totems) that shield the truly nasty dementors (the darkest creatures to inhabit the planet), from shape-shifting animagi (witches or wizards that can morph into animals), to love heals all as the most powerful force in the world—the bridge to the Potter universe is small for me and the edges between these worlds of the magical to the mystical are blurred if not non-existent entirely.

Even now, after many years in energy healing and mystical spirituality, even though there is an increasing amount of scientific evidence that it is all real, the magic of it still takes me by surprise, filling me with the awe of a child watching a gifted magician.

When I see orbs pop into my room during a healing session and descend into my client, I catch my breath, as I do when I look at a digital photo I took of my parents' living room on Christmas morning and see that six orbs have shown up and graced us all with divine energy. When I witness a time warp or the colors of an aura pop into view, I am left dumbstruck by the illusory nature of what seems solid and real to my senses. Even yesterday, I was cleaning out my daughter's bedroom when the unexpected happened. I took one of the framed pictures off her wall to clean the cobwebs out from behind it. As soon as I lifted the hanging wire off the nail it was delicately balanced on, a dark energy swooped out from behind the picture and arced up into its dissolution. Instantly, I thought, *Boggart! Harry Potter!*

Boggarts aside, I was pretty sure I knew what that dark swooping energy was. I called an intuitive friend of mine and he confirmed my suspicions—an elemental. An elemental, in my usage, is an energized thought form. Anytime someone thinks a thought (remember: everything is energy, even thoughts), an elemental is created and sent out into the world. Most of the elementals floating around out there are pretty innocuous. This is because they don't have a lot of emotion or passion put into them. They're like weakly deflated balloons—not much power there. However, if someone has a thought they feel very strongly about, either positively or negatively, they energize that thought form or elemental, and it can do a world of good or a world of harm. It can exist on its own and can even seem to have a mind and life of its own.

When a group of people forms elementals collectively, whether consciously or unconsciously, the power of the elementals is amplified, equaling more than the sum of its parts. I once did an energy clearing in a house where someone had died of cancer. There were literally dark, heavy, dense balls of fearful thought forms hanging around in the air of various rooms, stressing everyone out in the house and depressing them. So too, with the opposite: I once entered a prayer room for a very spiritual, very progressive group of nuns. The space in that room was filled with lightness and peace. You could (or at least I could) actually see the clarity of the energy there. So, just like in Rowling's fantasy, a spell for good or for ill—an intention of thought plus intense focus and emotion—can indeed produce a visible, tangible, noticeable effect in your life and in your home.

Thus, returning to that swooping dark energy behind my daughter's picture on the wall, someone had probably greatly disliked the picture and an elemental "stuck" to it. This is partly how karma works. What we send out comes back to us. Thinking positively about yourself and others can quite literally heal better than the best charm spells Nurse Madam Pomfrey could ever do. Thinking negatively about yourself and others can feel like an attack and even harm a susceptible victim. The power of your thoughts and emotions cannot be underestimated. Neither can the power of love as JK Rowling has shown so beautifully and magically, time and time again.

Questions for Reflection: When does magic show up in your life? What negative thought can you change today?

Part Six
~Of Place, Time, and Money~

The Right House

A couple of years into my first pastorate at a small historic church in New Jersey and a few years into mystical experiences that had begun after my dark night of the soul (aka The Summer from Hell), I began to feel an overwhelming urge to move back to Seattle. Now in general this was not unusual. I did not enjoy the Joisey culture at all—way too hostile. I don't know if you've ever had grocery clerks cuss at you when you ask them, "How much is this soda?", but this type of thing was a daily experience in the Garden State and I was eager to get back to polite Seattle. All of my west coast friends from Princeton Seminary had already high tailed it back to the west coast as soon as they could after graduating, and I wanted to join them. However, I had survived for eight years in the "armpit of the country" and had pretty much resigned myself to staying for at least a few years longer.

Until that is, in late 1998, when I started to *know* I was supposed to move back to Seattle. This new impulse was much stronger than any previous longing I had to return to my native land. It was much more like I *had* to go back. There was something I was supposed to do in Seattle. I didn't know what it was exactly, but I knew I had to move back soon. I confess: I didn't know how I knew this. I just did. I told this to my husband.

"What? Why?" he said.

"I don't know. I just know I'm supposed to be in Seattle and we're supposed to move back there."

"How in the world am I going to run my business in New Jersey from Seattle, Monica?"

"I don't know. All I know is we're supposed to move back. We don't have to make any decisions yet. I know this is your decision, too, but just keep an open mind, okay?"

"Okay," he resigned himself. I'm sure he knew he was doomed. I rarely get adamant about anything so he knows when I do, something big is looming on the horizon.

We had already been planning a spring trip to Seattle in early 1999, so we decided to keep our eyes open and see what happened when we were there.

As it happened, during that trip my husband came upon a couple of business possibilities in Seattle that really got him excited to move back. Plus, he too was very anxious to leave New Jersey as he didn't like the culture there either, and we both wanted our children, one five and one two at the time, to grow up knowing grandparents and cousins, who all lived in Washington.

So the first thing that drew me back to Seattle in the first place was this knowing that was persistently pushing me, compelling me to persuade my husband to relocate back to the gorgeous Pacific Northwest.

The second thing that happened was a little more concrete. Even though I was a minister, my entire life I had always found it hard to pray with words. I'd stumble and stutter. I was not what they call a "prayer warrior" by any means. For worship services I wrote out my entire prayers and read them. For me, there was no other way. However, for the past few years, I had—I thought—"invented" for myself a different way to pray. I now know it's a very specific type of contemplative practice that St. Ignatius described in detail centuries ago, but I had come up with it for myself without any knowledge of St. Ignatius' writings at the time.

What I discovered was that I could pray visually by coming up with a spiritual landscape in my mind's eye and presenting a situation or question to God symbolically with a picture. And as you know, a picture is worth a thousand words. I found I could communicate much more deeply and quickly with God this way and after a little practice at this, I discovered that "new" pictures, pictures I was not intentionally imagining would pop into my mind that would answer my questions to God. So back in New Jersey when I *knew* I was supposed to move back to Seattle, I started asking God where I was supposed to work.

In my mind's eye I would start out with a beautiful landscape. I would feel myself jump off of a cliff and start flying like an eagle over this landscape and then just see where the "movie" in my mind went. I would see myself flying over a lot of country and I would always land at this certain destination. I could see a light brownish church surrounded by lofty evergreens somewhere close to a shoreline. Within this church building was a small group of people arranged in a circle. I could see they were of a different skin color than me but I didn't know what ethnicity they were. I seemed to understand it was an ethnic church that met in this larger church building. I also could see one of the men in the group. He would always look at me with his dark eyes. At the time I assumed the dark eyes were simply ethnic eyes, but now in retrospect I know it was the soul-dark eyes of the senior minister of the hosting congregation.

Regardless, I would see these images every time I prayed visually. I didn't really know what it all meant except that I knew this was the church I was to look for in Seattle because I was supposed to work there.

So when we did, in fact, move back to Seattle in July 1999, I started looking for this church. Oddly, a friend of mine from seminary, "Jennifer" had been an interim associate minister at a church that seemed to fit the description perfectly. It had a small Hispanic congregation that worshiped at the church and they were looking for a full-time associate pastor. I, however, was not interested in working a full-time pastorate. I wanted a part-time position. And I assumed from what I had seen when I had prayed that perhaps I was to work with this Hispanic congregation doing some sort of cross-cultural ministry, a deep passion of mine.

However, when Jennifer asked the senior minister if he was interested in hiring someone part-time to work with the Hispanic congregation, he said, "No."

Jennifer told me, "They're still looking for an associate though, Monica."

"No, not interested in full-time. Thanks, though. Keep me posted if anything changes."

In the meantime, I was still trying to force my way into a dream job at a dream church while looking around for the church that fit the description I had seen in visual prayer. Nothing came about. No church seemed to fit.

Then mid-summer 2000, after the dream job had inexplicably fallen through for about the fifth time, my daughter, then age four, piped up that she wanted to go to pre-school full-time. This was a complete one-eighty because up to that point she did not seem ready at all, but I thought, *Hey why don't I look at full-time pastorates if she's ready to go to school full-time now?* I called my friend Jennifer and asked if the church had filled the associate position yet.

She told me, "No, they're having no luck at all finding an associate pastor."

So, I quickly put together my resume and drove to the church to drop it off. I couldn't believe it. When I pulled into the parking lot, I felt spooked. The church looked exactly as I had seen it in visual prayer—light brownish, surrounded by tall evergreens, and the town it was in had the word "beach" in it no less. It was also very close to the shoreline of the Puget Sound. Twilight zone chills ran up my spine. Moreover, this church was only a block away from where my son was already attending a private school and another block from where my daughter could attend full-time preschool. I had never seen the church during my son's tenure at the private school as a first grader because the church was behind the school with lots of trees in between and I had never had any reason to drive behind the school.

But the rest, as they say, is history. I very quickly "clicked" with the ministerial search committee. Fortuitously, even more things worked into place and within a few weeks I was offered the position. I was told I had the highest rating of everyone they had interviewed for the position.

But this wasn't all. There were more factors that had fallen into place with hardly any effort on my part. In the spring of 1999, when we were planning on moving back to Seattle, I looked regularly on the *Seattle Times* website for house rentals. In the middle of May, one such rental I saw described looked ideal. I called a friend of mine who lived not too far away from this rental and left a message on his work voicemail asking if he might drive by this rental house on his way home from work and see if it looked decent. I knew this area of Seattle was in great demand to live in so I didn't know if the rental would still be available, but I was crossing my fingers anyway.

An hour later, he called me from his cell phone from inside the rental house! This is how our conversation went:

"Monica, I got your voice mail when I was at home for lunch so thought I'd drive by the rental house on my way back to work, and I saw the front door was open. So I just went in and the landlord's agent was already showing the house to someone else. She said I could come in look around. I'm here now. Do you want a room-by-room description?"

"Sure! That's amazing! Thanks, Dave!"

And so, room-by-room, he walked through the house and gave me a description that sounded perfect to my ears. Plus, he told me the house was only a half a block away from Discovery Park, a wonderful tree-filled park in Seattle with a magnificent view of the Puget Sound.

"Dave, this sounds perfect. Can you get an application form or something for us?"

"Monica, the agent wants to talk to you. I'm just going to give her my cell phone so you can talk directly with her."

I then proceeded to tell the agent that we were moving the first of July and we definitely wanted to apply to rent the house.

"Okay," she said. "I'll hold it for you."

"Ummm. Come again?"

"I'll hold it for you."

"You'll hold it for a month and a half?"

"Sure!"

"What do I need to give you in order to do that?"

"Oh," the agent said, as if it were no big deal at all, "Just send back the paperwork after your friend faxes it to you and that'll do."

"Don't you want some money down or something to hold it?

"No, we'll settle up after you move here."

The only thing I could talk the agent into doing was signing a paper that she gave to my friend confirming everything she had told me over the phone. I wanted to get this unbelievable promise in writing.

And it happened just as she promised. She held the house for us for a month and a half with no money down and we didn't even have to pay for that month and a half. They also allowed us to bring our pets and we had a great year in that house.

But after a year, the owners decided to put the house on the market to sell so we were again looking for a rental. We were not going to buy until I had found a job. This time, something no less miraculous happened again. Right away, I found a great funky house with a roof deck and a view of downtown Seattle, Mt. Rainier, and the Puget Sound. Upon showing me the house, I told the landlord's agent we would like to apply, thereupon which he gave me the keys to the house.

"Excuse me, don't you want me to fill out some paperwork or something before you give me the keys?" I queried.

"No, just fill the application out when you get a chance," he shrugged.

"Don't you want some money down to hold it?"

"No, we'll take care of everything later."

I don't know if these sort of things have ever happened to you when trying to rent a place, but when I told an aunt of mine about it she said, "Monica this kind of thing just doesn't happen. I've been trying to help my son get an apartment and just to go in and look at the last place, we had to give the rental office our driver licenses and they wouldn't give them back to us until they had gone through the apartment after us and made sure we didn't steal anything or damage anything. I can't believe they gave you the keys with no money and no paperwork."

When I told my next-door neighbor how we got the rental, she said, "Honey, you have angels working for you."

I was going to need them. The next few years as a whistleblower were harrowing to say the least and yet the Divine and the angels arranged two more perfect houses for us during that time. The first of these two was a dream home Tudor with an established herb, rose, and fruit garden. Even though we were not first in line for the house and our bid to buy it came in lower than those in front of us in line, the owner decided she wanted us to have it anyway as I was a minister. During those intensely difficult years, the house was like a retreat center for me.

In the tumultuous end we had to sell the house after enjoying it for four years, but the next rental emerged again as a miracle. I happened to be driving through an unfamiliar neighborhood, saw a rental sign in front of the house, and called the rental agency. The rental agent told me, "We only just put up that sign an hour ago. When would you like to see it? I could be there in a half an hour."

"Great!" I said, amazed again at how housing seemed to fall into our laps with next to no effort on my part. I toured the house, signed the application, and we've been here ever since.

The lesson I've learned from all of these housing miracles is that when you follow your direct knowing—your Truest Self and its inner divine guidance—the universe will take care of the details: handing you keys without rental contracts if necessary, to see that all of your needs are provided for. If you are fulfilling your soul's contract, even landlords will bow down to the divine purpose working itself out in your life. Truly we have nothing to worry about. Ever.

Questions for Reflection: How have you been provided for miraculously? Try visual prayer today for something you need guidance about. What is shown to you? How can you trust this in your life?

Time Warp Travels

"The distinction between past, present and future
is only a stubbornly, persistent illusion."
~Einstein

I loved the movie, *The Time Traveler's Wife*. Usually, I like the
book better than its film version, but in this case, the vivid
images and beautiful screenplay were far more captivating to
me than the more morose verbiage I endured when reading
the book. The film was truly romantic—a story of love
transcending time. Metaphysically, it challenged our linear,

material view of time, in particular, our emotional and mental attachments to the belief that time goes in one direction only.

This linear view of time is uniquely western. In many indigenous traditions, time is circular or spiraling; in eastern traditions, time is an illusion; and in yet others, time is only spoken of in past and present tense (no future) or of only the ever-present now. Current science posits that the space-time continuum creates a "fabric" of reality that started at the Big Bang and we move through the unfolding fabric objectively in part, as can be marked by the interplay of moons, planets, stars and suns, and subjectively in part, as when we perceive time as going "fast" or "slow" depending on our activity or concentration level.

However, in this chapter, I am talking about something altogether different than time travel, the orbital marking of time, or its perception, no matter how subjective. I have been living with time warping, where time literally disappears and is "lost" or expands and is "created." I have experienced both frequently, and of late, of increasing frequency. I know I am not unique in these experiences as other healers and intuitives comment and remark on these things as well.

In healing sessions, time warps occur on a regular basis, either by collapsing or expanding. This has been evident not only in individual sessions, but especially in group sessions. When everyone in a group session exclaims, "That was an hour? It seemed like ten minutes!" Then I know it's not just a warped perception of yours truly's mind, but a group experience that everyone can validate.

Recently I did a healing session with a woman. During the session, I did very little overall, not even having her do the breathwork I teach, since she was in such extreme pain. I did do some energy medicine and recalling how much I did with her, I'd say I did about twenty minutes worth. However, I started to feel like I had done enough for her and so I glanced down at her wristwatch. I was really surprised to see that an hour had gone by, so I stated, "Well, it's gone by fast, but it's been an hour."

To which she opened her eyes, looked at her watch herself and said, "Really? An hour? That was so fast!"

All this is to say it still could be a matter of subjective perception rather than actual time warping. Except that I know better. For instance a few days ago, I drove my son to his friend's house and then I drove back. This is a six-minute trip total, ten minutes max if the traffic is bad (which it wasn't). However, when I got home, having not paid much attention to the elapsing time, I walked in the door and my daughter said indignantly, "Where have you been? You've been gone a long time!"

"What?" I said, "I just dropped off your brother at his friend's and came right home. Why? What time is it?"

I then looked at the clock on the wall and saw that twenty-five minutes had gone by since I left the house. Where did those fifteen or more minutes go? I confess: I'm not sure. I assume I unconsciously entered another dimension while driving and time warped for me.

I regularly experience this bizarre time warping in dreaming, though I cannot with any accuracy detail the actual minutes gained or lost. One time after waking up in the morning and looking at my alarm clock, I fell right back to sleep and dreamed a Big Dream to use Carl Jung's designation of such epic wanderings of the consciousness during sleep. The story went on and on, like a drawn out movie, and it felt like hours had gone by before I re-awoke with the full story still completely remembered in my head. I looked at my clock. Two minutes had gone by. Weird.

Moreover, I have experienced even odder happenings that make me feel as nutty as my husband's trail mix before I castrate it. I "hear" things before they actually happen. For example, I hear a knock on the door and go and open it only to see no one there. Then I hear the knock again a minute or two later and I return to the door to see that someone is there this time. Or I hear someone I know call my name and that person is nowhere in my vicinity and then within a few minutes that person does enter my vicinity and does indeed call my name. These could just be mini-premonitions. But because it seems to happen with such insignificant things and usually in less than five minutes of elapsed time, I believe I am experiencing the overlap of the "dreamtime" and the "waketime" as indigenous people call it. The dreamtime happens nearly simultaneously, a duplicate world that is the energetic doppelgänger of the one we experience in the "real" material world, but it is just a little ahead of it. So, in the merging in my consciousness of intuition and "reality" I begin to experience both worlds in my waking time, where time is elapsed and simulated.

It may be that that time is spiraling, linear, subjective, objective, and many others things altogether, working at different levels for various reasons. I am certain, though, that time is fluid—moving and flowing, stopping and going—for reasons beyond words and explanation. All this is to say is that ultimately, time is a *mystery*—exactly the subject a *mystic* majors in.

Questions for Reflection: How does time happen for you? Have you experienced time warping? Do you use time or does time use you?

"I Have My Ways"

One day in early September 2008, with the national polls indicating the McCain-Palin ticket was ahead for the first time in the United States presidential race, I did some serious ~~praying~~ complaining to God during my daily contemplative walk. Not to offend any Republicans who may be reading but I had a strong intuition that a President McCain and a Vice President Palin would spell a capital M-C-P-A-I-N for our country, so I thusly informed God of my foreknowledge, in case God was, you know, hanging out on the other side of the universe birthing stars or something and had totally forgotten about us here in the good ol' U. S. of A. (In retrospect, I laugh heartily at the audacity of some of my prayers.)

"God, if McCain becomes president we're going to have a global economic meltdown. I know there needs to be some serious cleaning of the house with money in our country, but if our country goes, so goes the world. The poorest of the poor countries will plummet and then there will be untold suffering of even more millions if not billions. I know this is all a divine drama unfolding but those suffering don't often have the spiritual luxury of realizing this amidst all of their pain. I don't think you should allow another Republican to be president. God, what do you think you are doing???"

At that very moment I heard these words both from outside of me as well as from inside my own head, audibly and firmly announced: "I have my ways."

I then felt a strong, magnetic energy above and behind me to my left, and I turned just in time to see an enormous bird approaching me and then fly right over my left shoulder. My mouth dropped open, large enough to drive a semi-truck into, I was so taken back by the ginormity and proximity of whatever kind of bird it was. Its wingspan was huge, its feathers brown and mottled. A nature-loving friend from Montana insists it must have been an immature eagle. "If so," I replied, "It was a giant one." (Considering the picture I found online afterward of an adolescent eagle, she's probably correct.) As I walked on, I watched in awe as it flapped away in front of me with its exaggerated flexuous appendages. Regardless, the words given followed by the giant bird's fly-by helped me release my concerns and return to a place of deep inner peace.

Little did I know at that time, though, that a near global economic meltdown was about to occur in a matter of days, before anyone had the political luxury of voting. During the catastrophic money crisis that did ensue that September, I was able to maintain my deep inner peace, partly because, I confess, I had next to nothing to lose. I had already ridden the money horse during my several year saga when we lost everything except for one car and our clothes and furniture. So, except for the possibility of our ATM cards suddenly not working, the stock market plummet had little potential effect on our financial lives. But I believe the near meltdown is what helped shift the election away from the ticket I intuited would bring more of the same financial doom.

Although I was rather peaceful during the steep slide down into near economic collapse over those few weeks of fall '08, I did experience two unusual phenomena. Often I would awaken at 6 a.m., PDT, with a painful knot in my stomach. Not being personally affected much by the crisis, the macraméd knot in my stomach was not coming from any stress I was experiencing. How could it be? I was sound asleep. Rather, I intuitively knew I was connecting with the collective fear and anxiety of the country's group consciousness right before the stock markets would open on the other side of the continent at the corresponding time—9 a.m., EDT. The stomach pain would wake me up abruptly and I would have to get up, walk around, do some breathwork, and consciously return to my center. Only then would the muscle tension ease so I could return to bed. I noted that on weekends and when the markets eventually stopped bottoming-out and stabilized, I never awoke at 6 a.m. with a knot-in-the-stomach.

The other odd phenomenon occurred whenever I would see a governmental or political figure on TV who was speaking about the crisis. I would start to sense their energy: the fear, the dread, the anxiety, or the very shut-down heart. I would have to intentionally stay in my own awareness and energy, keeping my own heart open, and then send the person a lot of peace and love.

However, the main reason I was able to remain calm during that catastrophic financial storm was because of the Voice which spaketh "I have my ways" and the Power that didst launcheth an eagle's flight plan into my path on that day when I dispatched a passionate plea for divine intervention into the presidential race. If I were tempted into angst I would remember what I knew: the Divine is working out healing through deconstruction as well as reconstruction. I am always safe. There is nothing to fear. God has God's ways.

When the Divine speaks, even though the seeming reality appears dire, one is reminded that only God is Real. Only Love is Real. All else is fleeting and temporary. When God speaks, no matter what the circumstances, one knows of the firm foundation that God who is in all is working out Divine intentions for healing, even if that means a massive decline of the world's markets. Maybe these trying economic times that persist three years later are required to derail an even more serious threat: the actual meltdown of our planet vis-à-vis global warming.

In uncertain times it can be so easy to move away from our center—away from our knowing, away from our beingness. And yet, it is precisely at these times, that it is so important to stay in our center. You may have heard of the controversial "hundredth monkey effect." Some scientific studies have shown that once one hundred monkeys learn a new skill, multitudes of monkeys around the planet, are suddenly able to do this same skill, though they haven't been taught the skill directly or interacted with their enlightened kin. Meaning? The entire collective consciousness of monkeys shifted when one hundred of them learned something new. More recent studies have shown that when even ten percent of a population believes something very strongly, the idea spreads very quickly into a majority opinion. Even in a small room with just one or two other people, scientists have demonstrated that the brain of the strongest person in the room—the one with the most focused mind—will begin to entrain or alter the brainwaves of the others in the room to match the focused brainwaves. All this occurs with no words spoken.

Thus, the more you can stay calm in the storm, the more those around you will pick up your peaceful vibes. The more those around you stay in peace, the more people around them stay in peace. Pretty soon a one-hundred-person or a ten-percent shift can cause the entire human collective consciousness to shift into this new way of peace. The next time you are tempted to fret, remember the One who commands the eagles and the waves, the Voice who says, "I have my ways. Fear not."

Questions for Reflection: When you experience lack, what feelings arise in you? What works for you to return you to calm when you are feeling anxious? When has someone else's calming presence made a difference for you?

Gaia and the Energy of Place

When I was being psychologically tested as part of the requirements to become an ordained minister, one of the questions the counselor asked me was, "What fairy tale fascinated you as a young child?" On the spot I couldn't think of anything but soon after the testing was over, I recalled Hans Christian Anderson's classic, *The Princess and the Pea*. I knew from my own training in spiritual care and counseling at Princeton Seminary, that favorite stories from early childhood could indicate strong archetypal or personality patterns in a person.

It makes sense. In the tale a prince seeks a princess bride. None are found to be suitable. However, one night a young woman shows up at the castle door soaked to the bone from the chilly downpour. She claims to be a princess so the queen sets up a test. She puts a pea at the bottom of twenty mattresses and twenty down covers and invites the young woman to sleep on the top. In the morning the woman complains that she didn't sleep at all as something hard in her bed kept her tossing and turning and even making her body turn black and blue. This proved her princessness and she was married to the prince.

Being an empath, you have to get used to feeling things others don't. As a child I had no idea that one of the reasons I felt so miserable a lot of the time was that I was intuiting everyone else's stuff and it was overwhelming to try to cope with it all. This ability to feel others' energies has only been enhanced as the years and experiences have accumulated. When my cat, Snuffles, is sick to the stomach, I can feel the nausea. When my client's have a block in their body and energy, I can locate it by feeling it first in my body.

Needless to say, I avoid large indoor malls. And hospitals. And middle schools. Walking through them feels like I'm being bombarded simultaneously by a cacophony of energies—similar to sitting in the band right in front of a couple of crashing cymbals, a dozen bass drums beating, and a few trombones blasting—only not as pleasant. I have learned how to not let external energies throw me off my own centeredness through conscious intention and focus, but it's simply easier and I think wiser not to force my energy through the challenge unless absolutely necessary. However, being an empath entails more than just feeling other people's energy—if that isn't enough to deal with on a daily basis. It also involves tuning into the energy of place.

As I was driving from Seattle to Portland last summer for a book-signing, I encountered a new energy. I was considerably south of the big urban sprawl that connects Seattle, Tacoma, and Olympia, in an area typical of much of the Pacific Northwest I-5 corridor: evergreens, occasional green meadows, and freeway exits dotted with a few small mom-and-pop stores and gas stations.

Without any forewarning, I drove into what felt like a bubble and instantly the thought popped into my head that I had entered a Native American area. I looked for signs and evidence but saw nothing. There certainly wasn't a reservation nearby and even the mom-and-pop stores didn't indicate historical roots in Salish culture. What there was, however, was a meandering river nearby suggesting that perhaps the freeway was connecting with an old trade route. I took note of the town's name and memorized it for research back at home.

Late that evening, on my way back home from Portland, I wanted to see if I felt the same thing again. It was about 10:30 p.m. and very dark. I would not be able to identify the place by sight and familiar markings at all and had forgotten on the way down to look at the mile posts, so I really didn't have any idea how many miles from Portland this area was situated— all the better for simply trusting my intuition to tell me. And again, it worked. I felt myself drive into a bubble and had the same "going back in time" to Native energy feeling. It wasn't until I had driven to the north side of the town (two mom-and-pop stores = town) that a sign and the meandering river revealed that it was the same town I had driven through a few hours earlier with the familiar feel of the energy.

How curious! When I got home it was well after midnight and so I went straight to bed. During the night, I had a long, vivid dream. In it, a Native American man showed me how they fished in the river with baskets and gathered and washed berries there. I have never had a dream like it. When I woke up the next morning I was very motivated to find out if this town had Native history and was delighted to find it did. It was not a permanent village, but it was where the Nisqually people would take a trip every year from farther inland and set up a temporary encampment so they could fish for smelt and gather berries there, just like in my dream. Perhaps it was such a long-standing tradition that the consciousness of the Nisqually was still active in that place. Since it is not a very highly populated area even today, the collective energy of white settlers hasn't recorded over the Nisqually energy.

It caused me to reflect more deeply on the energy of place. Even when I was much younger and traveling abroad I could feel the energy of a country as the airplane would circle its descent towards landing. I could feel the oppression of women in Japan before I landed, though I couldn't put my finger on it and name it at the time of the airplane's descent. Until, that is, a couple days later when we were walking through Tokyo at night and we all saw the multitudes of older married men out with young, single women and I knew that was the oppressive energy I had felt in the airplane. It's not that husbands cheating on wives doesn't happen elsewhere, but there its acceptance as normal built a strong energy that I could literally sense in the air. (Ironically and gratefully, women are safer in Japan than in most western countries, even able to walk around by themselves at night without fear of any violence.) I could also feel the intense fear of Israel/Palestine when I lived there for a summer, and it took me several weeks of living back home before I stopped repeatedly looking over my shoulder at the slightest trigger. I had become so accustomed to living in that paranoia— justified paranoia or not.

More recently, I have noticed that even smaller places have an energy that can be picked up on. For example, at a local grocery store, I noticed that every time I walked through the store's south door, I had thoughts of stealing. This is not normal for me and I also noticed that I did not have these thoughts when I walked through the store's northern door, or into other stores for that matter. I surmised that either a number of people had stolen through these doors and therefore their thieving thoughts had remained in the energy of the door, or the store managers were so afraid people were stealing through that door that their fearful thoughts had remained in the door area. Soon after I drew these conclusions the store started closing this door at night and only kept the northern door open. A sign also went up that stated, "Shoplifting will be prosecuted to the full extent of the law."

Our thoughts have power. Our collective group thoughts have even more power. Be careful what you think! If you notice you have a negative or limiting thought, don't buy into it, just say, "Delete!" to your brain so it can reprogram and not tune into the negative thought energy coming from your subconscious, from somebody else, or from whatever energy of the place you are in.

The earth, Gaia, has her own energy of place. Humans have done a thorough job rewriting over the energy of harmony and balance that is inherent in Gaia's energy. Gaia can heal Herself, though. The question is whether we will join or hinder Her in this endeavor. Gaia is ready to work with and help us. She can feel us and our thoughts. The only times scientists have ever recorded a spike in the normally uniform geomagnetic resonance levels of the earth's energy since they have been recording such things, occurred on two occasions: after Princess Diana died and after 9/11. Gaia felt our collective, intense thoughts and emotions and noticeably responded.

What this does not mean is that negative thoughts and emotions are more powerful than positive ones, but that intensity is key. I experienced this firsthand when I was out walking my dog, Ruffles, a kindly Golden Retriever who lets his squirrel and crow friends share his dog food without moving a muscle or making a sound. As we were about to round the corner of our block and head home, I could see that a vicious dog, who occasionally visits the neighborhood to be pet-sat by a relative, was loose and coming straight for us, charging and snarling all the way. As soon as he turned the corner and was almost to us, I held up my hand in front of me and with a forceful energy yelled, "NO! Go home!"

The dog then looked like it had run headlong into an invisible brick wall as he abruptly stopped in a contorted fashion, started to whimper, turned around, and ran all the way back to his temporary home, tail between his legs without looking back at us.

Something similar happened when I met with a certain official person during my saga. I didn't know whether I could trust him or not—he was an ambiguity to me. As he came toward me to greet me, his body, too, suddenly looked like it had run into a brick wall situated right in front of me. He stopped short and his body bounced back a bit, ricocheting off of whatever he had "hit." He then looked at me shocked, like, *What the heck was that?* He didn't try to greet me again, and stayed well back from me during our meeting. I assumed either my thoughts or my angels had erected some type of forcefield to keep me protected in a precarious situation.

When I have held water blessings at the edge of the Puget Sound, Gaia has responded visibly and viscerally. On one occasion as our ceremony ended, a golden rainbow—something none of us had ever seen before—arced out of a cloud above us. Just as we ended the ceremony on another occasion, the sky—which had been overcast all day—broke open to the blazing of the setting sun and the illuminated rising moon. Even a bystander noticed the amazing synchronicity and remarked on it. At the beginning of yet another such ceremony when we spoke our intentions to help Gaia, a surge of energy rose up from the earth into our feet and legs. Gaia had heard our heartfelt prayers for Her healing and She let us know She had heard with a little local spike just for us.

Say a prayer for Gaia. Say a prayer for humanity. Send Light and Love to your community, to the whole planet, and to all life Gaia cradles.

Questions for Reflection: When have you picked up on the energy of a place? How did you feel? What connections do you have with Gaia, Mother Earth? How can you nurture those connections in your own place?

SynchroniCity

I have just had another encounter that bemused, if not amused, me. A tall, slightly graying gentleman who looked in his right mind in every way, passed by me as I walked to the Starbucks near the small mall in our town. As he approached me, he looked at me as if he knew me well, and asked pointedly, "Are you done? Did you finish?"

I continued walking past him as I stammered, "Ummm?"

Then he said, "Did you have coffee?" As if he thought I had just been at Starbucks when in fact I was on my way there.

"No," I responded matter-of-factly over my shoulder as I stayed my course.

Not flustered in the least, he shot back, "Did you want some? I'll go and get you some!" as if we spoke to each other every day about such things and were in fact, well-acquainted.

Quickly turning around to him, I replied, "No, thank you?" I was unsure how to end this odd conversation and so, I turned back around. But by then the distance between our opposite trajectories was not optimal for dialogue and he didn't initiate another query.

A case of mistaken identity? Alzheimer's or perhaps mental illness after all? Perhaps. However...

I once had a young woman come up to me in nearly the same place as this quirky pre-Starbucks conversation. As she was walking in the parking lot, I was on the sidewalk near her, and out of the corner of my eye, I saw this woman turn and look at me. She then sprinted towards me, stopping right in front of me to block my forward progress.

Her next move was to start screaming like a Beatles' groupie with her hands in the air, shaking her shoulder-length blonde hair all around. She then yelled, "Oh my god! Oh my god! It's her! It's really her! Oh my god! [Insert more screaming here.] I can't believe it's you! Oh my god! Oh my god! [Scream. Scream some more.]

Needless to say, everyone within a mile radius had turned to look and see what celebrity had graced this suburb with her presence, only to be confused when they saw me. *Who is she?* they were clearly thinking.

The woman, infatuated with whomever she thought I was, took a good look at me as I stared back at her with extreme confusion, then seemed embarrassed by her very public outburst, turned away just as suddenly as she had come, and went back to her car and left.

Again, mistaken identity? Alzheimer's and dementia were totally out of the question this time as she couldn't have been older than her late 20s. She certainly looked sane and healthy. And to be sure, I don't have any Hollywood doppelgängers that might cause such a reaction in anyone.

If these were the only two instances, I might simply shrug my shoulders and move along, bewildered with only speculative answers. However, considering several other instances of total strangers who act, well, strange, around me, I confess, I have wondered if it was I who had the mental imparity.

Many times people I know I don't know have waved at me furiously while smiling at me with big, toothy grins that would rival the Cheshire Cat, or pointed at me and laughed uproariously when they saw me, even though I was in no way looking or doing anything worthy of humor or an exceedingly friendly gesture, let alone worthy of any attention at all. My tendency in these situations is to check over my shoulder to see if they're perhaps reacting to someone behind me. But no, it becomes obvious they are reacting to me. I've also had strangers walk right up to me and give me specific answers to questions that were rolling around in my head at the time. How could such specific answers be given from strangers again and again often in the exact same wording and language I had used in my silent queries to the Divine?

At first, my puzzlement over these frequent oddities increased until my mystical awakening occurred and I knew who I and everyone else was. We are, each of us, a form of the Beloved. Knowing this, I saw that all of these encounters are, in fact, explainable though still jaw-droppingly astounding. These strangers were simply me, the transSelf in each and all, experiencing itSelf—like looking in a mirror and talking to yourself—a synchronicity of Divine Order.

When the Self meets the Self and recognizes itSelf, amazing things can happen: ear-to-ear grins, laughter, familiar dialogue, synchronistic answers, even screaming rock-star worthy admiration. It can be accompanied by a strong feeling, similar to what you feel with a soul mate—the déjà vu feeling of recognition and completion—the feeling of wholeness. It is not an owning of the other or a subjecting of the other to seduction or domination to come under your control—it is simply an acknowledging of the awareness of Oneness embodied. Even in encounters of seemingly random open hostility, I see aspects of my Self resisting the reunion into that Oneness due to fear and so I offer compassion.

Awareness facilitates the re-membering of all of the individuated parts of the Divine back into their True Unity. This synchronicity of Unity isn't just with people, but with all life—trees, animals, and birds all are facets of the One Jewel as well. During healing sessions, it's amazing how Nature shows its own unique face. If I tap into an energy store in someone that is holding some repressed anger, my dog in the back yard will start barking. When I facilitate a guided meditation having someone merge with the Light, the sun will break through the clouds at that very moment. (Recall that I live in Seattle where cloud cover is a near constant, so that a sunbreak, as we call them here, is truly noticeable.) When an energy block that is waiting to be cleared isn't yet obvious to me, a bug of some kind will suddenly begin flying around me at the same spot that corresponds to where the block is on my client.

Once while working with an ankle injury, just as my client released the stuck, murky energy the sprain was holding, a large, shadowy crow flew up from out of the bushes right outside the living room window my client was lying beneath. Her sprain was totally healed. Similarly, a blue jay will cackle, a hawk cry, a squirrel come near, just as my client makes a profound shift or has a significant insight. I can't imagine doing healing sessions without a window nearby to see the synchronicities happening in Nature with energy work.

Such encounters happen with so much regularity that it makes me wonder if I should rename our municipality. I confess: I'll be submitting an address change to the postal service. I live in SynchroniCity, WA, USA, the best place on earth!

Questions for Reflection: When have you experienced synchronicity? Did it include a feeling or awareness of Loving Oneness? Can you remember this feeling and hold it in your heart today?

Money Crumb Trails

This money issue of ours just doesn't seem to want to go away. Everything in my life that I lost because of the *My Karma* saga has rebounded or been reborn into health and wholeness—except our finances. I must confess again: It is a mystery to me why it is taking so long to reap the abundance I know I am and that has been promised to me by the Divine. I have worked the lessons to their core, and yet still we live day to day or week to week, at best, month to month. After years of this and years of applying for jobs to increase our income and being unsuccessful, I admit to being completely stymied at times as to why this cycle continues. (For the answers maybe I need to consult the book: *The Whistle-Blower's*

Guide to Eternal Unemployment.) Even now as I write, my husband's current job is possibly on the chopping blocks in two weeks with no other job prospects on the horizon, and no unemployment benefits to back us up. This is a job that already isn't paying a living wage and we are again behind on bills. I learned quite a while ago not to be stressed or anxious about money issues, but frustration and discontent? Well, I'm still working on those.

At a similar impasse like this a few months ago, I was imploring the universe in the privacy of my own car, "Why? Why are we here again? Why is abundance simply not flowing for us?"

I then pulled behind a car in a parking lot at the bank where I was going to juggle some money to keep us afloat. It was a newly purchased car and the temporary license could barely be seen through its darkened back window. However, in the license plate holder, the driver had put in a fake handwritten license on a piece of paper where the real one would eventually go. It read, "KARMAAA."

Laughing instantly at the wicked humor of the universe, at least it confirmed my suspicions that a larger picture than I could see had a hand in our circumstances. Even when the answer is not what I wish it to be, it is always comforting to me that at least the universe is answering—specifically, immediately, and often tongue-in-cheek.

It's also reassuring to me that in the midst of the lack and scarcity we struggle with, the universe is continually showing me when money is going to come in by leaving me "money crumb trails." Usually I find a penny and a dime—eleven cents—right before an unexpected check comes in the mail, a surprise financial gift is granted, or an out-of-the-blue business contract is offered. Eleven is a power number meaning divine perfection. It is also one my personal omens giving me guidance that all is perfect in the divine plan for me, and that our money matters matter and are being watched over by forces outside my awareness and control. For example, the rental house we had to move into fast when our finances collapsed a few years ago was confirmed to me as the right house at the right time when I realized the numbers were all elevens and multiples thereof: the house number ends in 22, the street number ends in 88, the zip code ends in 55, and our phone numbers end in 1144 and 1155.

I will confess, that even with all these signs I still have momentary lapses of faith, trust, and knowing. I complained once to the universe, "Really, is it only pennies and dimes that you can bring me?" Right after I said this out loud in the car—I have a lot of conversations with the universe in my car—I parked and got out to go into the grocery store. There on the sidewalk was a coin. I picked it up. It was a peso. [Smirk.] In another similar situation I asked the universe the same question and added: "Why not fifty cents sometimes?" A few moments later I spied a coin on the floor of the grocery store I was in during my silent lament to God. I found it was a frivolous game token with "50 cents" stamped on it. Be careful what you ask for. The universe is listening.

After reworking and editing this book recently, when we were again facing possible personal economic doom, I drove to a nearby grocery store to do some errands. I pulled into a spot in the parking lot only to then notice that I'd parked right behind what must have been the same auto that had the handwritten KARMAAA license plate months before, because there was the permanent one in the license plate holder—the photo of which is at the beginning of this chapter. The universe was unambiguously reminding me (and my stubborn, disabled faith), that the money issues we are dealing with yet again, are part of this karmic lesson in our lives.

Sometimes the universe even acquiesces to my protests at the crumbs, and I'll find hoards of nickels and quarters in addition to pennies and dimes show up. Right before a book-signing trip to Canada I found five dollars in Canadian change—helping me pay for dinner in Vancouver, B.C., that evening. Just now, I took a walk to take a break from writing and there in the middle of the road was a penny and a nickel. Again and again, the universe lets me know that no matter what, it is invested in my well-being, every penny of the way, karmaaa notwithstanding.

P.S. While doing the final edits of this book, our money issues healed (finally) on 11-11-11, no less! It came about after I was able to hold my knowing that I AM abundance, no matter what the circumstances looked like, and I was able to hold this knowing without any negative feelings (like anxiety or tension), any negative thoughts (like complaints or skepticism), or any negative energy (like frustration or discontent). At all. It was an extreme spiritual lesson and I confess: I'm grateful it's over!

P.P.S While doing the final, FINAL edits on this book, I noticed for the first time that the expiration date on the KARMAAA license plate photo is 11/11!!

Questions for Reflection: What is your relationship with money? How can you let more love and trust flow through you regarding your finances? Money is simply a very dense form of energy, so issues with energy usage in general (time, thoughts, food, etc.) can show up easily in money situations. Where are you being guided in these areas? If you would like more help in this area, please see the Resources section for more information about the e-course I created based on all of my learning around money and finances.

Part Seven

~Of Healings and Blessings~

Eagle Eye

There is nothing like having a firefighter for a father. Firefighting was something my dad did like other people do knitting or golfing. It was his hobby. He brought home his paycheck through other employment, but for all of his adult life (nearly fifty years), he has volunteered at the local small-town fire station, even rising to the heralded position of fire chief. For most of my childhood, we lived just a half a block away from the fire hall. When the alarms would blare in the middle of the night, we would all wake up just in time to hear my dad tear out of the house with the front door slamming shut behind him.

I do not think the other firefighters knew that my dad slept in his underwear. I also do not think the other firefighters knew that is all my dad ever had on underneath his firefighting gear. Because my dad would never have sacrificed precious time to get dressed, he kept all his gear at our house—boots, and suit right beside his bed—unlike the other firefighters who kept their gear at the station. He did this so that, upon hearing the first moan of the alarm, he could just jump from his bed into his boots, pull up his straps, pull on his coat, and race down the street to get to the station first.

But even if it had been revealed to the other firefighters that my dad was fighting fires in his undies, he would have kept doing it. This was one lesson my firefighting father taught me: some things are more important than what other people think of you.

Living with a firefighting father was also a bit like living with Steve Irwin, the Crocodile Hunter, as a father. Things that most people would consider incredibly dangerous were for him an adventure not to be missed. We could have capsized in a fishing boat in twenty foot swells in the Straits of Juan-de-Fuca, because my dad wanted to catch a fish that he had hold of on his line. We could have slid off a cliff on the Al-Can highway with two feet of mud under our truck and fifth-wheel trailer because my dad wanted to try and drive down the slippery slope, so to speak, to see if he could make it. Other drivers had jackknifed their semi-trucks and gotten stuck in their vehicles all the way down that steeply graded hill. Fortunately, my dad's love for extreme adventure is matched only by his extraordinary skill and expertise in driving and handling machine equipment and we made it safe and sound in both cases.

Anyway, I learned to live with a sense of danger, with a keen awareness for always being on alert. For example, my dad would wake my brother and me up in the middle of the night for a fire drill. We were then to demonstrate that we could climb out my second floor bedroom window and down the TV antenna in our pajamas. My dad had installed the TV antenna right outside my bedroom window and he had chosen an antenna with ladder-like steps so it could function for the express purpose of a fire escape.

To this day, I will not sleep on the second floor of a house without checking to see how I might escape in the middle of the night. I also dutifully change all the batteries in my smoke alarms, installed in every room, on every floor, twice a year.

The other lesson I learned from my father, or perhaps it was just a trait passed down through the genes, was to keep an eye on the lookout. My dad has always had an eagle eye for spotting things. We would occasionally race off the main road on a leisurely Sunday afternoon drive in the mountains, because he had seen smoke in the distance where there should be no smoke. Or, more frequently, we would suddenly pull off to the shoulder of a highway, and begin going in reverse, because my dad had seen a good screwdriver or other tool lying beside the road he thought he could use. My dad could spot things the rest of us couldn't because we weren't paying attention or even looking.

I don't think my dad ever misspotted a thing. Where he had thought he had seen misplaced smoke, he had indeed found an unmistakable fire. For in the firefighting world, where there is smoke, there is fire.

I have found this is only too true in the spiritual world as well.

If a client has an energy that's not in alignment with their Truest Self I'll spot it. If a client says something that's not quite the truth, it reveals itself in their energy, their tone of voice, their eye movement. This works for systems too. I can see the systemic shadow almost as soon as I walk into a group or gathering. There is no judgment here or even calling out the dis-ease or misalignment, just a noticing and acknowledgment internally on my part until the "smoke" reveals itself in its own time, or the person or system wants some help figuring out why their life energy is draining away or sacred purpose is being sabotaged. Having an eagle eye is an excellent tool for being a mystic healer.

An eagle eye works not just for smoke and fire, but even more for the essence of light that is at the core of all created and manifested reality, no matter the "smoke screen" shielding it. The core star or divine spark shines luminously as a beacon at the center of each person's being, and orbs of supernal light dance around us, drawn to music, dance, joy, love, especially on holidays and at festivities. In photos of powerful healers orbs of light swarm en masse, and healing energy shows up as large parallelograms, rectangles, and waves in the air.[1]

Skeptics call the orbs of light that appear in new digital photography "specks of dust that shine off the flash and rebound on the lens" (according to Wikipedia). This may be true in some cases but this doesn't explain why these orbs show up a lot in pictures of nature, around healers especially, or as large geometric shapes during healing sessions. (Skeptics, respond please. Skeptics? SKEPTICS?? *Cue the crickets.) Plus, I can see those orbs of light with my own naked eye. They pop in during healing sessions, but I see them every day as angels, spirits, and other divine beings of light bringing in gifts of healing energy to someone who needs help. Heaven is around us all the time.

Not only is it true, then, that where there's smoke there's fire, but where there is anything, anything at all, there is always light. Always. I confess: I'm glad for my dad's eagle eye. Without it, I wouldn't see the dazzling displays of divine beauty in everyone, everywhere. Truly the world is a stage or even a smokescreen. I invite you to look deeper.

Questions for Reflection: When have you spotted something others missed? Did you trust what you saw or dismiss it? How can you honor your own eagle eye today?

[1](To see some of these photos you can find them on my facebook profile under "photos" and "orbs." facebook.com/monica.mcdowell)

The Sword in the Stomach—The Knife in the Back

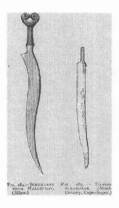

Fig. 284.—Scramasax from Hallstadt. (Hälms.) Fig. 285. Scramasax. Danish (Ninth Century, Copenhagen.)

"They will come back -
come back again
as long as the red earth rolls.
He never wasted a leaf or a tree.
Do you think [God] would squander souls?"
~Rudyard Kipling, *The Sack of the Gods*

"I see a sword being thrust through your son's stomach."

This is what an intuitive friend said to me one day when I told her my son was struggling with some digestive issues. Her statement cohered with something another intuitive friend had told me a couple of years prior to this. He had said, "Your son achieved enlightenment in many lives and he paid a heavy price for trying to share his enlightenment. He has also been in many battles and wars and is carrying several mortal wounds from these past lives in his energy."

I confess: I didn't exactly know what to do with this information. Should I tell my son what was said to me? Should I hold it until such a time that I deemed he was ready to hear it? Should I never speak of it and let him learn it all on his own time, in his own way? He was in his teens, after all, and living in a society that at least in the public sector scoffs at the esoteric. I was loath to burden him with information that might make him feel at odds with the rest of his peers. Or, perhaps it is better to say, *more* at odds with the rest of his peers. Being empathic, aware of energy on a level I have only in recent years become in touch with, I do not know how he makes it through his day, surrounded by the intense and oftentimes chaotic energies bombarding him daily in his high school. He must feel like he's on the outside looking in at the social games and politics all too common with kids, aware, so self-aware amid the many souls who haven't even begun to contemplate such a thing as energy, let alone consciousness.

I decided to withhold the information for the time being and just play it as it came. My main concern was getting my son feeling and functioning better. He was extremely bloated, in pain, and just felt terrible with a capital "T." We had already determined he was mildly lactose-intolerant, but taking dairy out of his diet did not alleviate his symptoms much. Something else was aggravating his system. We finally concluded that gluten was the culprit and upon taking that away, he did begin to feel mildly better. However, his digestive system was not healing very fast, and he had schoolwork to catch up on and sports activities to attend.

During this time I was referred to an intuitive acupuncturist from China whose skills were apparent as soon as my son got on his treatment table. That man knows a body like a tightrope walker knows a wire. He quickly read several things and using what I can only call Extreme Acupressure followed by acupuncture with a few needles, the energy blocked in my son's stomach began to move.

"Mom, I feel like I'm going to throw up," he groaned as Dr. Chen nodded like this was a good thing.

I, too, knew it was a good thing for when blocked energy begins to move through the body it can feel much like stagnant, murky water. So, I encouraged my son, "Just hold on. It's the backed up energy starting to unblock. You'll feel better in a bit."

And, indeed, in a few minutes his stomach had settled. For the next week his symptoms, though much improved from the acu-treatment, were still lingering and giving him some discomfort.

About a week after this treatment, he went to bed one night and within a few minutes, he got up again. He emerged from his bedroom, holding his stomach and said, "Mom, I don't feel so good." All hunched over, he walked over to me where I was sitting on the sofa in the living room.

He looked like he felt much worse than he had in quite awhile and I asked him, "Do you want me to check your energy?"

He nodded and so I got up and quickly used my hand to scan the energy in front of his body, starting in front of his head and going down toward the energy in front of his stomach. As I reached his stomach, my hand "hit" something. I put "hit" in quotation marks, because obviously there was nothing there materially. Energetically, though, was a different story. My hand felt something large and something metallic protruding out of his stomach. Each time I touched it to connect with it, he grimaced and moaned.

Clearly, it could have been the sword my friend had "seen" and told me about several weeks prior. It had emerged in my son's own energy awareness in its own time and now I had a choice to make. Do I tell him or not? I felt intuitively that it was time to clear it and from my experience as a healer I know that giving the person some information about what I was sensing could help to clear the energy much faster.

So I made my decision on the spot and repeated to him what my intuitive friends had told me, but I framed it as such: "You may or may not believe this. That's okay, but I want to tell you that a couple of months ago one of my friends said she saw a sword being thrust into your stomach. This would obviously be referring to a past life since nothing like that has happened in this life. It's up to you whether you want to believe it or not. Another friend told me you had been in many battles in past lives and had mortal wounds from them. What do you think?"

His eyes enlarged to the size of dinner plates. He turned and looked at me and nodded.

"This story resonates with you then?" I questioned.

He nodded again and then as I set my intention to clear the energy of the sword with healing Love and Light, something happened that I've noticed in many clients when I discuss with them an intuitive hit I've received about a connection between a past life and a present day situation. My son's eyes glazed over and rolled upward a bit in their sockets, almost like he had gone into a mini-trance. Perhaps this happens with people as their souls connect to their larger story in order to help clear the energy being brought forward to the present time. I quickly cleared the energy and the sword disappeared from the field. It took about five seconds.

I asked him, "Do you feel any different?"

He seemed to come-to and said, "Yeah, that feels a lot better." With that comment, he went back to bed and fell asleep quickly. The next day, his digestive symptoms were almost gone and the next day they were completely eliminated (Har!), no pun intended.

Think of it what you will.

A similar event occurred with my husband's aforementioned back injury. At an appointment with the chiropractor, I wandered over to the table my husband was lying face down on as he waited for an adjustment. I looked around to make sure no one was watching and casually put my hand up to feel the energy in his lower back just to check in and see what was going on with it. As soon as I did that, I "felt" a knife go through my hand. It certainly wasn't nearly as painful as if a material knife had gone through my hand, but it wasn't exactly a comfortable feeling, either.

I quickly and discreetly cleared the energy of the knife from his back. The stabbing spasms that so far the chiropractor had been unable to fix ceased after this time.

I confess: I do not believe I am unique in my gifts. Far from it. We are all interconnected. We are One. Each of us intimately and eternally exists as an emanation from the Source of All. The infinite energy that has manifested as material stuff contains vast fields of information. Anyone, as part of the One Love, has the potential to tap into it at any time. Doing so can heal yourself or someone else. It's a simple as that.

Questions for Reflections: Have you or anyone you know experienced some type of healing beyond current medical science? If so, think back on it and reflect on what its teaching is for you right now. If not, Google words about "spontaneous healing" and see what stories speak to you. Are you a healer?

A Backside Blessing

This past summer, our family took a series of day trips around our state. On one trip we visited the Snoqualmie Falls. Thundering down the mountainside, the craggy rocks hidden by the foam rising from the misty water, it is a sacred site of the Snoqualmie Native people. Ernie Barr, Jr., son of the late Snoqualmie Head Chief Ernie Barr says of the Falls: "That's where Heaven and Earth meet. And the mists...that roll up to Heaven carry our prayers and our hopes and our dreams to the Creator of us all."

Opposite these spiritual Falls, there is a lookout gazebo perched perilously on a jutting ledge. As we stood there amidst tourists from around the world, gazing down at the cascading liquid river, the energy of its essence reached into me, mesmerizing my body with its pure force. I felt clean, renewed, revitalized. So much so, I confess I made a spontaneous decision that was in retrospect not exactly wise.

During my saga, my body's health disintegrated. For a couple of years, taking a casual walk around the block was impossible without becoming so over-stimulated, my heart's nerves would shock me at night from being fried. Gratefully, I have been the recipient of many, many healings—both spontaneous ones from heaven as well as gifted ones through healers. I can now enjoy long walks as long as I stay hydrated throughout. However, hiking up a long, steep hill is still a dubious activity. And thus, my spontaneous decision to hike with my kids down to the lower river to see the waterfall from below wasn't exactly wise for two reasons. One, I had no water with me and it was a hot August day. Two, there were warning signs posted at the top of the trailhead and all along the way saying, "Steep climb back up." The energy of the falls had so enthralled my body I was sure I could make it.

Intuition bells, however, were chiming in my head: *"You have no water. You have no water to drink with you. You have no water!"*

What do you do when the Emergency Broadcast System's alarms on television and the radio begin to bleep and the rote recording blares, "This is only a test. This is only a test. If this had been an actual emergency..." Personally, I turn the volume down to mute as fast as possible, which is exactly what I did to the intuition bells' repeated chimes in my head as well. I was so excited to get to the river's edge and view the falls from their entry point in order to contemplate a full scope perspective on them, and so hoping for more adventure, that I began the descent, mute button still on.

Excuse me, but let me take this moment to remind you to pay attention to public service announcements, and flight attendants when they remind you of emergency procedures before take-off, and to warning alarms going off in your head. I confess, I also continued to ignore every actual, non-intuitive warning sign posted beside the trail that kept declaring the steepness of the climb back up. If you've ever repeatedly turned off the "snooze" button after a few more moments of rest in the morning, well that was me all the doomed way down: snoozing, refusing to wake up to the signs. I kept telling my stubborn-in-denial-self that many, many people, in much worse shape were making it back up so I, with all my newfound energy, could too.

As my offspring and I neared the end of the descending winding mountain trail, I began to ponder the alarms in my head that I had ignored to my potential demise. It wasn't just steep. It was a long, distant way back up that mountainside and I was unprepared for a hike in hot weather. But now, it was just a matter of a few steps and we would arrive at the bottom. If we turned back now, it would waste the effort I had made. Might as well go the entire way to at least see the falls from below, and so make my doom worth it.

Just as we neared the bottom of the trail, I spotted yet another cadre of hikers sitting by the side of the trail resting. It could be me in a few minutes. These were the least likely looking hikers. Dressed in traditional Hindu garb—colorful sparkling bedazzled saris and bejeweled slippers to boot—I wondered how hiking was even possible. They looked ready to go to a wedding feast, not in the least ready to hike up a dirty, steep mountain trail. Maybe on the way back up, I would join them on the impossible journey.

One Hindu woman's energy in the group pulled my eyes to her. She, too, sensed my gaze turning to her and she looked my way. I noted two talakis (red dots) on her forehead, one large and one small. I didn't know the significance of two—still don't after Googling it—but I know that sometimes they are beauty marks, and sometimes they are "third eye" marks. Since she had two, perhaps she had one for each. Anyway, it was her energy that drew my attention first, and when our eyes locked in the knowing of Oneness, the smile she gave me was as pure and refreshing as the waterfall's essence. Whether it was a sign from the Beloved to counterbalance the warning signs in my head and along the trail, I wasn't sure, but I took it as such anyway. And then, as I passed her, I felt the energy behind me light up like sparklers and burst into my back heart chakra. I knew instantly, she had given me a blessing—a backside blessing. Another sign? Again, I'm not sure, but if I hadn't hiked down that mountainside, I would have missed this backside blessing.

After feeling the full-on power of the falls crashing into the pools below, along with a rainbow gracing the rising mists, we ventured our way back up. Slowly. Very slowly, with many breaks and me kicking myself repeatedly for not bringing the water bottle I had left behind in the car (another instance of ignoring my intuition!) But I made it and that night I fell asleep quickly and easily with no symptoms of heart or nerve over-stimulation issues. Did the Hindu woman's backside blessing combined with the waterfall's sacred energy make the difference? Who knows, but I have humbly learned that grace rises from the mists even when the powerful crashing of doom threatens to undo us.

Questions for Reflection: When have you ignored your intuitive guidance? What happened? Did you receive blessings anyway? In what form? If not, what did you learn? Isn't that learning a blessing?

Energy Jell-O

I confess: Jell-O just isn't my thang. I don't think I've served it once as an adult—distinguishing me greatly from my mom and mother-in-law, who both make it for almost every family dinner meal. Just the sight of a Tupperware gelatin mold sends me into an instant stupor—faster even than the sight of a PTA meeting announcement. (I think I went to a PTA meeting once, a long time ago, when my eldest was in third grade. Maybe. I don't know. I have a vague memory of a gavel strike officially starting one and then I must have passed out from sheer boredom for I remember nothing else. Perhaps it was only a dream. Nevertheless, I have henceforth avoided all PTA. I might be allergic.)

Because my mom makes Jell-O a lot, I ate it a lot as a kid. However, as an adult, I have only considered it solidified kool-aid, or, in other words, flavored, colored sugar water that's squishy. Gelatin may be important to the diet—Jell-O, not so much.

Jell-O was ruined for me once and for all at a family picnic where one of the relatives brought a three bean Jell-O salad. I. Kid. You. Not. As I peered down into it from above I surmised that it appeared to be lime Jell-O with garbanzo beans and lima beans added—the third legume I couldn't distinguish through the gelatinous green density suspending the beans in its midst. I refused to put any of it on my plate let alone eat it. I still have nightmares. I've since boycotted all Jell-O vegetable salads—right along with PTA meetings.

What I love about Jell-O, though, are the old Cosby commercials that always emphasized the jiggly, wiggly, giggly aspect of it that kids love. It is that jiggly, wiggly aspect of Jell-O that came to my mind a couple of years ago. I was driving to the Taste of India, my fave restaurant in Seattle, to meet a friend for lunch. Taking the winding back-street arterials through Craftsman and Tudor imbued neighborhoods—this was the fast way to the hole-in-the-wall eatery due to the Interstate tending to clog up right before noon—I made my way onto a one-way road that would lead me straight to my human fueling destination. I instinctively slowed because it was a busy street near the University of Washington with many harried pedestrians trying to cross streets and impatient drivers trying to pull over and park curbside.

At one intersection up ahead of me, I saw a pedestrian standing on the corner waiting patiently to cross. There was no stop sign, stoplight, or crosswalk at this intersection to aid pedestrians in their attempt to traverse the busy thoroughfare. They either had to wait until traffic cleared or a car stopped. After noticing this pedestrian, the worst happened. The driver of the car right in front of me decided to slam on her brakes all of a sudden. It appeared she had seen the same pedestrian I had out of the corner of her eye at the last second, and without first looking behind her to assess the potential damage to the flow of traffic, decided to stop on a dime in order to demonstrate pedestrian-friendliness. She in no way needed to by law, by any means, for the pedestrian had not stepped off the curb or in any way indicated she was about to bound into traffic.

We in Seattle are often so polite it's exasperating. If you remember the Chip 'n' Dale chipmunks from cartoons, who when they were about to leave would inevitably argue, "You first." "No, you, I insist!" "Absolutely not, after you!" "My honor will not allow this!"—then you know what it's like at a four-way stop in the Emerald City. Not only are Seattleite drivers often stalemated by their own courtesy, they frequently create dangerous, traffic-crashing, death-causing scenarios by their so-called good manners. A woman was recently cited and charged for stopping in the middle of the Interstate to chase ducks off the urban freeway. She caused a chain-reaction, three-car-crash that included a semi-truck. Great eco-civility. Terrible acumen. Think *Portlandia*.

Anyway, as I was slamming on the brakes like the driver in front of me in order to try to avoid rear-ending the absurdly polite driver, I also blared my horn. I confess this was just a teensy bit out of anger at the driver in front of me who had been so treacherously kind, but mostly because I knew there were cars behind me in my lane and I wanted to alert them that I was stopping super fast in case they weren't paying attention. Although I was able to stop without hitting the Chip 'n' Dale driver in front of me, as I was screeching and blaring to a halt, I peered in my rear view mirror to ascertain if any of the drivers behind me were aware I was stopping rapidly and wouldn't you know? I could see clearly that the driver directly behind me was totally distracted, looking off to her right as if searching for an address number on one of the buildings.

She then, upon hearing the blasting of my horn, turned her head and looked to see me stopped right in front of her still moving car. Her mouth dropped open and at that point I knew I was going to get hit for sure. So I turned away from looking in the rear view mirror in order that my neck and head were positioned straight ahead for the impending impact. I tried to both brace for the crash as well as relax into it so none of my muscles were straining to prevent injury to the extent I could.

And in an instant her car hit. *Hard.* Everything went into slo-mo. I heard the crunch of my car's rear fender, and felt and somehow saw the shock waves begin to travel from the rear of my car towards the front. But as those shockwaves reached me, I could perceive on some level that I was surrounded by a big bubble. The shockwaves hit the outer bubble's edge behind me, and as they moved through the bubble and towards my body, I realized I had turned into what I can only describe as energy Jell-O—for when the shockwaves got to me they went right through me, wiggling and jiggling through my body without the slightest resistance. As soon as these tsunamic energy waves moved out of the gelatinous corpus mass I had somehow been transfigured into, and then out of the front of the car, it was over. The bubble dissolved, my body returned to its standard non-Jell-O density and time and space returned to "normal."

I was totally fine. I hadn't been thrown forward or backward and my neck hadn't even whiplashed the tiniest bit during the collision. My body had no aches or pains, not the next day or thereafter. However, my car ended up needing $1500 worth of repairs and the car of the driver who had plowed into the back of me was totaled by the crashing force that blew her airbags. She took a trip to the ER but a few months later at a court date for her ticket, I saw she was physically fine from the accident. Her insurance company covered all of my car's repairs and I required no follow-up medical attention.

Why was I transformed in this moment? I confess: I have no idea. I was rear-ended once before and once after this Jell-O-energy-inducing accident, but nothing mystical saved me from whiplashing those two times. All I know is that this particular time my body turned into a less dense substance, and energy traveled right through it. Perhaps it was just to show me yet again: I AM being watched over. I AM protected. I AM an energy being. Quantum physics tells us that matter, what we commonly think of as "solid," is really not. Our subatomic particles are energy or light, and only appear to "set" when observed. Otherwise they are indeed something like Jell-O. For whatever reason, this hidden, mysterious reality oh-so spontaneously shows itself at times I have no control of.

Just the other day, I was driving my daughter home from her school flag team event. We were on a highway going 45 mph when suddenly I felt a familiar cinching around my waist—a sign I've come to know that means my helpers on the other side are connecting with me. Immediately, I was growing. I felt like I was blowing up like a balloon, encompassing the car, the road, the trees, the entire neighborhood. If it turned out not to be a mystical experience, I was going to be peeved because I was gaining weight a thousand times faster than when I was a chocolate-ice-cream-sucking, pregnant moo-cow. As I grew, my vision expanded higher: I could see it all and I knew my awareness was leaving the car.

I thought loudly, *STOP! Wait until I'm home, please. I'm driving!* For I realized in a split second that if this expanded state of consciousness continued to expand, I was going to lose my reference point to the road and wouldn't be able to drive safely anymore. I began running my energy into the earth, to help ground myself and stay connected to the reference point of the car. *STOP! STOP!* I continued to yell in my head, knowing from experience that my thoughts are heard easily from the other side. And then gradually I returned to my small body driving in the car, making it home safe and sound.

I believe these moments are simply given. They are gifts—glimpses into our larger world—to remind us who we are. My helpers on the other side seem to want to remind me of that while I'm driving, for some reason—at times to keep me safe, at times to help me learn to keep myself safe. Their reasoning often leaves me baffled, but by catapulting me again and again deeper into the mystery that births us all, I am forced out of my own mental Jell-O molds into a greater ability to walk through my day and sleep through my nights aware, awake, and alive. I am so grateful.

Questions for Reflection: Where have you been given glimpses into the larger reality of Spirit? How does this help your consciousness grow, expand, and awaken?

Healing Transmissions

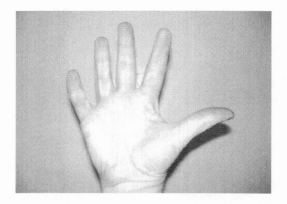

I have to be careful where I sit these days. Apparently, my energy is affecting others in bizarre ways. The other day I was in downtown Seattle waiting for my son to finish a food handler's test for his job while I whiled away the time at a nearby Starbucks a few blocks away. After ordering a chai latte, I found an oversized armchair—typical of a Starbucks coffeehouse—empty, sat down in it, and started into a thick novel I had brought along to occupy me. Within a few seconds of sitting down in the chair, the man in the chair next to me, very much in the vicinity of my energy fields, rose and left. I couldn't necessarily chalk this up to my energy, although I confess this sort of "get away from her quick"

response to my presence does seem to happen somewhat frequently. Body odor, you ask? Not typically a problem of mine. However, what I believe I could chalk up to my energy was what happened when the next person came and sat down in the same chair that had just been vacated.

He was a tall young man, in his late 20s perhaps, dressed in casual downtown attire and like me, had a book in hand to peruse while drinking his grandé-sized beverage. After he sat down and began to read, I noticed out of the corner of my eye that he would periodically reach over to the round coffee table in between our chairs, pick up his latte, take a sip, and put the latte back down.

I figured if anything were going to happen between us it would happen in less than five minutes. Sure enough. As he continued to read he gradually changed positions in the chair. At first he had sat down in the chair in the proper sit and read position: back straight, feet squarely on the ground, rear-end squarely in the seat. As the first couple of minutes started to tick by, he gradually shifted so he was sitting somewhat sideways in the chair. Again, nothing I could necessarily attribute to my energy as perhaps he was just settling in and getting more comfortable.

But his shifting didn't end there. He continued to scoot sideways and then began to bend his knees, one leg at a time, eventually lifting his legs up and off the floor. It continued until, no joking, he was completely on his left side, back rounded over, with legs curled all the way to his chest, arms circling his knees, head bowed. Here was a grown man, professional, well-groomed, and handsome, well over six feet tall, totally scrunched up in his chair in a full fetal position.

Uh-oh! I thought to myself, *I wasn't expecting that.*

I watched him some more as he tried to read his book in what looked to me to be a very uncomfortable position, given his size relative to the chair. I realized on some level that my energy was giving him a sense of "mother love" and his body responded pre-natally to my presence. I honestly didn't think he could last long as a contortionist in this extreme repose and again, sure enough, after about a minute and a half, he abruptly lengthened out his body, got up and left. Just like that.

Oh, snap!

Another similar situation emerged at our annual neighborhood block party this past summer. About three dozen or so residential congregants stood in small clusters of chit-chat on a blocked-off street that sunny, appropriately named Sunday. I finished eating my served-up potluck dinner early, and so got up from the picnic bench I was sitting on to allow someone who hadn't eaten yet to have a place to sit in the limited spots available. One of the men who had been animatedly talking to others in the buffet line as he heaped various and sundry helpings of casseroles onto his plate, came and sat down in my just-vacated seat.

I was a wee bit concerned about who might sit in my spot. My energy is picked up quickly, if it is picked up, and I wanted to keep an eye out for any immediate reaction. Observing him carefully, though from some distance so as not to be noticed by him, I confess: I wasn't surprised to see that as he began scooping food into his mouth, "it" happened.

With lightening speed, his facial expression changed from one of light-hearted eagerness in his food, into grief. His eyes were watering and his mouth quivering. It was clear he was not having a reaction to spice or choking on food. The intensity seemed to escalate quickly and I thought it looked like he was trying very hard to get the sudden emotion of great sadness under control: like trying to slow down a speeding train by pulling on it from behind. I wanted to walk up to him and say, "Honey, it's going to take you on a ride. You can try your darnedest to dig in your heels but that way your emotional train is just going to beat you up something awful. Just get on for the ride it'll take you on. It'll be okay."

But due to my angst of freaking him out even more, I stayed put. You might be asking: Had he possibly picked up my sadness? I doubt it. I don't carry around that kind of energy on a normal day, having done a lot of clearing in that area. It's not to say it couldn't happen, just that it wasn't likely. Instead, I believe this person has had a difficult life; the emotions about which he manages to keep rather well repressed. Sitting in my energy, which tends to have an automatic clearing effect on people (even on the phone, over the internet, but definitely in person, too), it was bringing his "stuff" up to the surface to be released. And blast it all, if he wasn't having a difficult time stuffing that stuff back down inside him so he could continue to stuff his body with food. Hmmm. After a few minutes, the emotions seemed to subside and he continued eating quietly, without interacting with others as he had been prior to sitting down in my spot. I sent him some compassion and hoped that he had experienced some form of healing.

Not everyone will take to a spontaneous healing this well (cough, cough). This spring I was watching my son's track and field events from a local school's bleachers. After awhile, I noticed that for a radius of about six feet extended around me, the bleachers were completely clear of people, even though the rest of the bleachers in this section were full. My energy seemed to be keeping people out through no intention on my part. I also noticed that the only people who ventured at all into this twelve-foot diameter circle around me were kids. They'd come up, sit down, scooch up really close beside me, stay for a few minutes, and then get up and leave. It was curious. Adults, however, were totally staying away. Maybe a deodorant change is in order.

Several minutes later, however, a middle-aged couple came and sat on the empty bleacher seat right in front of me. As soon as they sat down, I instantly knew there was going to be an energy event. The man (okay, I'm seeing a trend here!) of this couple had a rather huge block in his heart. I could feel his stuck and stagnant energy in my own heart. I also knew either I would need to leave or he would. It was just too heavy for my own health. But I had been practicing setting an intention to stay in my own energy regardless of the energy of the people around me, so I decided to try it in this challenging, heart-stopping energy.

Silently, I said to myself, *I'm staying in my own energy*, and immediately my heart's chakra energy responded by spinning rapidly in the optimal clockwise direction. Three seconds after my heart began whirling faster than a pinwheel in a hurricane, the man abruptly stood up and motioned to his wife, who got up after him. They then moved to the opposite end of the bleachers, as far away from me as they could get without leaving the bleachers.

Alas. I guess it wasn't his time to experience a healing. It can be one of the more challenging aspects of intuition—knowing someone desperately needs a healing—but having to let them go and walk their own path. We all choose to learn the hard way sometimes. It is simply not for me to judge.

I have noticed these energy transmissions taking place lately not just through contact or shared space. These energy transmissions can be passed through objects—underscoring the popularity of talismans given from teachers and gurus—through the human voice, and even through the soul-to-soul gaze between individuals. Even yesterday, as I began a class by introducing myself, a young woman in the front row burst into tears. I hadn't said anything that would provoke an emotional release—in fact, far from it. I had only stated my name and recounted a small bit of my educational background and out flowed her deep sobs. When she had mostly composed herself she shared that she didn't really know why she was crying. I had to apologize to her. Often when I start speaking people will experience deep emotions.

It doesn't necessarily matter what I say—it's just that healing energy can be transmitted through the human voice.

I've even witnessed an entire sanctuary full of a few hundred weep simultaneously as waves of energy surged through their midst for forty-five minutes during a sermon I preached. This was a sermon on healing that a few weeks before preaching it while I was driving home from work one afternoon, had been downloaded in its entirety into my brain—within a few seconds. Other times I've noticed that individuals want to look deep in my eyes and I can tell that something shifts. I don't know what if anything they've seen, because these gazes are spontaneous, short-lived, and without a verbal exchange. We just look in each other's eyes, I see into their soul, feel the healing happen, and off we go on our so-called separate ways.

Regardless of the persistent illusion that makes us believe we are separate, in Reality we are One. The energy that is in each of us is interconnected to everyone and everything and that energy circulates all the time whether we are aware of it or not. It flows most powerfully with Love—not the ooey-gooey Hollywood "I need you to complete me" codependence masquerading as love—but the never-ending infinite regard that Loves no matter what; the Love that is our true home; the Love that birthed each of us and will welcome us again and again back to the center of our mutual Beingness; the Love that heals all. Allowing Love to circulate more in your life—both giving and receiving—will spread that wonderful healing around and help us all shift into new ways of living Love here on earth.

Open your heart. Open your heart. Open your heart.

Questions for Reflection: When have you felt someone else's energy? What did it feel like? What has Love felt like to you? If you're not sure that you have felt it in your life, imagine what it would feel like to have all the Love you could ever want from everybody you could ever want it from for all eternity—no judgment, no disrespect, nothing negative, just total positive regard and welcome for you no matter what. Allow your whole body to feel this Love. When you have touched this place within pass it along to others and you'll begin to feel it more as well. If you would like, you may gaze at the picture of my hand at the beginning of this section or put your hand on the photo to receive a healing blessing.

Angel Rain

Healings are the norm around our house. It's hard not to heal when angels and other beings of light come in for clients and then hang out for awhile for the whole family to benefit. To be sure, healing doesn't mean perfect. Our family members have chronic physical conditions, we all have our issues, and we joke that living within my weird and wacky world, we should be investing in long-term therapy funds rather than college for the kids.

Healing for me means simply shifting to the next level. Theoretically, we can go on shifting for all eternity since the Ultimate is infinite, eh? (I grew up very near to Canada.) At our core we are already whole and thus, healing helps us reflect that wholeness more and more. This is far more about our soul growth than our body being free of any and all ailments. However, physical healings do happen around here. I confess, though, I'm not sure if my children are aware of how unusual it is that we can do healing.

Just the other day, I was suffering from a huge headache. I wasn't sure if it was from yet another energy download or just a crick in my neck that was making my cranium throb like there were sumo wrestlers beating on timpani between my ears. As the day went on it was getting worse. Later that evening I went to pick up my son from work. On the way home, the pain was distracting me from driving safely, so I asked my son if he would just rub my neck a bit and see if that helped.

He said, "Sure, mom," and reached over with his left hand and started rubbing my neck.

After about two seconds, he blurted out, "Oh, mom, you've got a block!"

He then moved his hand to the top of my head, closed his eyes, and it looked like he had started to meditate. In about another two seconds, I saw and felt an energy go flying out of my head, the new energy that was indeed trying to come in, did, and all of my headache and neck ache pain left. Just like that.

"Umm. Thanks!" I said to him. He'd never done anything like that before and I didn't know he could. I'd showed him quite some time before how to do energy clearings on himself, but I had not personally witnessed him clearing anyone else, especially so quickly and easily.

My daughter comes by the healing just as effortlessly. I walked her through a self-healing of her ear from an infected earring hole and she was able to clear it completely in twenty minutes. Even as a young girl, she had the know-how. She came home once from third grade and very off-handedly—

like it was the most normal thing in the world—told me about a healing she did on a friend of hers. They were playing on the playground outside during recess and my daughter's friend began complaining of a headache.

My daughter told me, "So I just did what you do, mom. I started pulling stuff out of her head, and all this spiky stuff came out. She felt a lot better."

One time I knew an angel was working on me and bringing me energy through the top of my head as I felt the typical energy pressure like a stack of books were piled on top of my head. At bedtime, I went to tuck my daughter in and she said, "Mom, there's an angel right over your head. I can see her face. At least I think it's an angel. It feels like an angel."

"I think you're right, sweetie. She's been working on me all day."

I love that this kind of thing is totally natural in our house.

The joy is also in spreading it to others—to clients, students, and readers—to anyone who's open. At a college lecture I recently gave on mystical spirituality, we had time at the end to do a breathwork meditation. About twenty-five students pushed aside their chairs, laid down on the classroom carpet, and started to breathe the pranayama yoga healing breathwork I teach. Healings happened on all levels. One young man, who had been told by doctors and acupuncturists that the nerves in his legs and feet had died and could never be healed, began feeling his legs by the end of the meditation. Several saw or felt their energy, others were moved to cry as they released emotional blocks, and many were curious. At the end, all I could feel and see was healing energy literally raining down on everyone, clearing out the old energy, bringing in new energy. It was beautiful! There were so many angels in that college classroom—it felt like angel rain.

The breath heals as it opens the door to God, the angels, and our souls. In Hebrew, the word for breath, *ruach*, also means wind and spirit. Other ancient languages have a similar linguistic connection to breath and life energy. We can live without food for weeks, without water for days, but only for a few minutes without breath. The breath is our closest connection to life, to the bridge between essence and form. That is why so many traditions advocate conscious breathing as forms of prayer and meditation. The breath heals!

There are so many healing stories I could share. Maybe it'll be another book. Healing is normal—if you live in my world. Healings may come differently than you expect, in their own time, in their own way, but trust. Allow the Flow to carry you and your loved ones, too. The Master Healer can heal us so far beyond our hope and imaginations, in ways beyond our thinking. Just set the intention to heal according to your highest and best and then get out of the way and hold on!

Questions for Reflection: What healings have you experienced or witnessed or heard about? What does this mean for you now? Practice deep, conscious breathing and learn a breathwork meditation if you have the opportunity. My website has meditation mp3 downloads that will teach you the breathwork I do. How does conscious breathing help you?

Epilogue

As a so-called mystic soccer mom, I am grateful that the two worlds of heaven and hearth actually function as one world for me. Heaven is not just other-worldly. It is within and all around us—all the time. The trick and the task is to be able to access this eternal state of beingness no matter where you are, who you are with or not with, and what you think you have or don't have. In holding this knowing you realize the Oneness that is our deepest truth, and this manifests the magic, the mystery, the mystique in your reality. To be sure, bringing this simple awareness into everyday routines is not always easy. In fact, I think motherhood may be one of the more challenging places to try to do this. It is, I dare say, easier to realize Oneness when you are off by yourself, supported by the charitable donations of others, away from the cares of the world, not having to deal with messes, crying children, bodies, cleaning, cooking, and the many other householding duties one must do or at least manage as a mom.

Thus, to all moms everywhere who have managed in some way to maintain any semblance at all of their own faith and spirituality in the midst of the multitude of the mundane, and even to pass it along to those in their care, I honor you. Gaia honors you. The Divine Feminine honors you. We sister women honor you and thank you. Namaste!

Preface to *My Karma Ran Over My Dogma*

Too Stupid to Smuggle

Mysticism is all about mystery and ever since I was a child, I have been fascinated by puzzles, riddles, mazes, crosswords, whodunits, anything where I have to figure out the smaller nuances in order to put the bigger picture together. So being a mystic is, I suppose, a logical unfolding of my childhood inclination. Naturally, the only book I still have with me from childhood, other than my Bible, is a Sherlock Holmes tome a friend gave me on my eleventh birthday. In the collection of stories, I was continually amazed at how from seemingly no clues at all, Sherlock was able to piece together the solution. But I also felt repeatedly swindled by Sir Arthur that the clues were shrouded in such a way as to be virtually impossible to put the solution together oneself. One had to wait until the end of the story, when Sherlock spelled it all out, to realize that there even were any clues in the story as to what was going on. The new BBC television series, *Sherlock*, as engaging as it is as a modern revisioning of the classic, has nevertheless stayed true to keeping the crime-solving just out of reach of the arm-chair detective.

Not so on the TV show, *Columbo*, with the bumbling detective played by the late Peter Falk. At least in those episodes, the clues were so obvious anyone could actively participate in the solving of the mystery. Another recent TV enjoyment, the *Monk* series, highlighted the obsessive-compulsive disorder of the detective. Although OCD is far from my reality—in fact, I could use a little OCD in the area of housekeeping—I still found I related to the persistent fixation that itched at Mr. Monk until he had solved the crime.

In time one begins to learn that in the solving of puzzles and especially mysteries, like Sherlock, Columbo, and Monk discovered time and time again, the spy is often too perceptive, too prying, too persistent, for his or her own good. A spy can very easily stumble into danger and usually does so without even realizing it, until it's too late. It's even more dangerous if God sends you to be a spy. You know you're in for a heap o' trouble if the divine Omnipotent has a mission impossible and you're the one chosen for the assignment. And you know you're in especially deep doo-doo (I am a mom), when you learn you've been commissioned as an undercover operative for the Almighty after the assignment has already begun! That's a *really* secret agent!

Anyway, I'm someone who doesn't lose the forest for the trees and can figure out the scope of the forest from the inside very quickly by listening, observing, and putting the pieces together. However, in other respects I truly am the last person God should've ever chosen for any type of detective work.

Now you might first be wondering why God would even send a spy. The Divine, of course, already knows what's going on. So, the spying cannot really be to let God in on anything that has escaped the All-Seeing Being. But for anyone who knows me, the bigger question is why God would send me. I am a stupid fool. I know it. God knows it. Pretty much anyone who knows me, knows that I often do stupid, stupid, foolhardy things—like my very first undercover adventure.

At the time, I was in my zestful evangelical years, which have long since passed me by. (The evangelical, that is, not the zestful. I'd like to think I have a few more of those zestful years left in me.) Nevertheless, please understand...

My college friends and I, while on a summer trip to East Asia to build a community center for a tribe in the Philippines (think spears and g-strings per my story above, *The Bat, The Cat and The Rat*), were recruited by a group to smuggle Bibles into China after we had left the Philippines. Well, okay, smuggle is an overly dramatic word for the actual situation. It reflects more how we felt about what we were doing rather than the reality of our circumstances. You see—taking Bibles into China was not illegal. So, technically speaking we were not "smuggling" Bibles, we were just "taking" them into China. However, "taking" Bibles into China wasn't exactly smiled upon by the communists either, so, if we were to be caught with the Bibles at customs, we might have had our bags confiscated and be turned back on the fast train from China. But that's the absolute worst of what could've happened to us.

Regardless, we felt like God's smugglers, like Brother Andrew of Christian legend. We were advancing the kingdom. We were risking it all for the sake of the gospel. We were fools for Christ. I, however, was the only Stupid Fool for Christ. For what I did at customs in Canton should have disqualified me from covert work for all eternity.

The people who recruited us to "take" Bibles into China split us into three groups. My friend, Tammy and I, formed the third group and we rode a train from Hong Kong into Canton. The strategy was to separate the groups so that if one group were to be found out, the Bibles in the other groups would still be safe—the divide and conquer strategy.

The train ride to Canton was tense. Holding tightly to my Bible-filled dufflebag, I stared out the window the entire trip ruminating on what misfortunes might await us. When we walked into customs in Canton, I was further intimidated just by the size of the building alone. It was a huge, warehouse-like, airplane hangar structure of communist-cold steel and barren cement. Inside, it was crammed packed full of thousands of travelers snaking their way through seven stations. Tammy and I made it slowly but surely through the first six stations and faced station number seven, the only obstacle remaining between us and a successful smuggling adventure.

Of course, station seven was also the most dangerous. At station seven the bags were scanned by machine then inspected by a communist guard, so if the Bibles were to be found out, this is where they'd find them. The scanning machine they used was an ominous looking monstrosity— much, much bigger than typical conveyor belt scanning machines found in American airports. It was taller than waist-high, with a fifteen-foot long and three foot wide conveyor belt that ended at two large, vertical scanning panels. On the other side of the scanning machine conveyor belt was a security-guard seating station where several communist guards sat looking intensely, even ruthlessly, at the monitors connected to the scanning panels.

Tammy and I decided the divide and conquer strategy would be a good idea for the two of us, as well. In retrospect this was pretty stupid foolish, too, because if only one of us got through, the other one (me) would have been left in Hong Kong all alone. After Tammy went through without any problems I waited in line behind several more people.

I was, I confess, zoning a bit, gazing off into nothingness and stressed to say the least, when I suddenly felt someone touch my elbow. I turned and saw that a communist guard was motioning it was my turn, and I realized he had touched my elbow to get my attention. Now remember, I am trying to take Bibles into China stealthily, without them being detected. So, suffice it to say, in a warehouse-size building crammed packed full of thousands of Chinese travelers, secured by machine-gun-toting communist guards, is not the best time in the world to climb up on top of a conveyor belt and stand on it. Yes, for some reason unbeknownst to me to this day, I thought the communist guard wanted me to get on when he touched my elbow and pointed to the conveyor belt. And so I did. It took me a couple of attempts to scale that communist monstrosity of a conveyor belt, but, hey, I did it. I then stood up on that fifteen-foot long belt and took a ride for all to see. It was a ride on the road to my greatest humiliation.

The really embarrassing part is that it didn't even occur to me as I was jerkily inching along that conveyor belt that anything was amiss. You might be asking yourself at this point, "What in the world was she thinking?" Good question. What I was thinking was, *Hmmm. I don't remember seeing Tammy get up here.* (Amazingly observant for a spy, don't you think?) I then noticed that the communist guards on the other side of the conveyor belt who were monitoring the scanners suddenly began to scream and yell (in Chinese, of course). I remember looking over at them, pondering their strange, erratic behavior. I was even a bit appalled at their outburst and thought, *Gosh! What's wrong with them?!* Immediately thereafter, the conveyor belt halted abruptly, meaning I halted abruptly too, and I reasoned with the utmost of rationality, *Oh, the conveyor belt's broken. That's what is wrong. No wonder they're screaming.* (Brilliant deduction, Sherlock!) But then, as I looked up again, I was genuinely puzzled to see that everyone in the entire warehouse was staring up at me, pointing at me with one hand, politely covering their mouth with the other hand, East-Asian style. And then the truth hit me like a bullet. I was a stupid fool.

After gasping from the impact of that sudden bullet of awareness, I started laughing at myself while I was standing up on top of that belt, which apparently gave East-Asian permission for everyone else in the warehouse to laugh at me too—including, no less, the communist guards. It was a common bonding moment for the few thousands of us. We all knew the same thing at the same time—that I was a stupid fool. Now, I certainly was glad I could provide such a measure of comic relief in communist China, even if it was at my expense, and at the expense of every blond-haired woman in America.

In a meager effort to try to regain some measure of dignity, I nonchalantly jumped down from the conveyor belt, trying to act as if nothing much had happened. I then held up my bag for the guard at the inspection station to find out if he wanted to have a look-see. When he realized I was trying to make a humble offering, all he did was motion with his hands. This is because he was doubled over guffawing and could barely breathe. Drunk with laughter, he kept waving his hands at me and then, finally, was able to get out a loud, "NOOOOO!" from his mouth. He was letting me know very clearly in English he was *not* going to inspect my bags, and he was waving me on and out the door of customs. He was of course thinking there was absolutely no need to inspect my bags because I was wayyyy too stupid to smuggle—or be a spy for that matter. So off I went, walking blissfully into China with my Bibles in my bag—my bag never having been scanned or inspected.

My friend, Tammy, whom I met up with at the door, was aghast. "What were you doing?" she yelled at me, "I thought we were had!" Seeing me up on that conveyor belt had convinced her we were going to be arrested. But apparently the absurdity of my act had caught the guards so off-guard, that Tammy and I and all of our Bibles were safe. I sometimes wonder if an angel or some other being from the other side, took over my brain and implanted the idea to get on the conveyor belt as a way to safeguard me from getting into big trouble in a foreign country. I mean, I'd been in many airports by that time in my life—I knew what the conveyor belt was for. At the time I was also a straight-A student, college valedictorian-to-be, Princeton Seminary grad-to-be, yada, yada, yada—certainly not a brainless blonde—evidence to the contrary notwithstanding. Alas, considering my history since that time of certain blips of clueless behavior, I doubt I can convincingly pin the conveyor belt mishap on an angel, let alone an alien, taking over my mind.

But, to answer the second question, why God would choose me to be a spy, all I can say is God works in mysterious ways, using even what is stupid-foolishness to the world to shame the wise. To answer the first question, why God would need a spy to begin with, you'll find it all in my first book, *My Karma Ran Over My Dogma*, the story that explains, step-by-step, my journey from whistle-blowing minister to mystic healer mom. Enjoy and thanks for reading!

Blessing

"When a sunbeam falls on a transparent substance, the substance itself becomes brilliant and radiates light from itself. So too Spirit-bearing souls, illumined by [Her], finally become spiritual themselves, and their grace is sent forth to others. From this comes knowledge of the future, understanding of mysteries, apprehension of what is hidden, distribution of wonderful gifts...endless joy in the presence of God, becoming like God, and, the highest of all, becoming God."

~St. Basil of Caesarea

Acknowledgements

I offer all my gratitude to the Divine Beloved and the helping beings and healing angels who are beautiful rays of the One Light. On this side of the veil, a more grateful heart I could not have for my husband and children who enrich me and teach me. I love you so much—no matter what.

Big thanks also go to:

My editor, Adrienne Koch, for her intuitive and excellent advice;

My publisher, Synclectic Media and Christian Mollitor, for believing in this book;

Kim and Cathy, who actually volunteer to read my first drafts, and who give me exceptional, priceless feedback;

My friends, clients, and readers for making my cup run over with every good thing;

The turtle who came to me in a meditation and wanted to be the totem for this book. I was astonished (and not astonished, too) to find out after the meditation that the turtle is the oldest symbol for Mother Earth, as well as the personification of goddess energy and the eternal Mother. The turtle embodies motherly compassion and the creative impulse and its shell resembles a soccer ball (in other words, the perfect totem for this book!);

And, Anne Lamott who visited me in a dream and gave me an awesome suggestion about adjectives! I hold her in no way responsible for the many adjectival failings in this book.

Appendix: Resources

Preface
McDowell, Monica. *My Karma Ran Over My Dogma: Lessons Learned by a Whistle-Blowing Minister Turned Mystic.* Seattle: Healing Light, 2007.

Hamilton, Marci A. *God vs. the Gavel: Religion and the Rule of Law.* New York: Cambridge University Press, 2005.
- A book detailing many legal cases having to do with church and state. It includes a summary of the precedent-setting federal ruling of my case.

Introduction
Millman, Dan. *The Way of the Peaceful Warrior.* Novato: New World Library, 1980.

Part One: Of Females and the Feminine
Estes, Clarissa Pinkola. *Women Who Run with the Wolves.* NY: Ballantine Books, 1992.

Part Two: Of Heaven and Bliss
McDowell, Monica. *You are Light: 8 Words Reveal Your Truest Self.* London: O-Books, 2011.

Schwartz, Gary E. *The Truth about Medium.* Charlottesville: Hampton Roads Publishing, 2005.

Documented scientific experiments with noted psychic mediums. See the book for a list of mediums he has researched and go to his website for more he is currently testing. http://veritas.arizona.edu/v_mediums.htm

Part Three: Of Marriage and Family

An excellent book on children's past lives is called (ironically), *Children's Past Lives* by Carol Bowman, New York: Bantam Books, 1997.

The books detailing the life of Daskalos:

Markides, Kyriacos. *The Magus of Strovolos.* Arkana, 1989.

—*Homage to the Sun,* 1992.

—*Fire in the Heart,* Arkana, 1988.

Sams, Jamie and David Carson. *Medicine Cards.* New York: St. Martin's Press, 1988.

Part Four: Of Animals and Nature

Ranquet, Joan. *Communication with all Life: Revelations of an Animal Communicator.*

Carlsbad, CA: Hay House, 2007.

Sams, Jamie. *Dancing the Dream.* NY: Harper Collins, 1998.

Part Five: Of Movies and Pop Culture

Wilber, Ken. *Integral Spirituality.* Boston: Integral Books, 2006.

—*A Theory of Everything.* Boston: Shambhala, 2001.

Part Six: Of Place, Time, and Money

Emoto, Masaru. *The Hidden Messages in Water*. Hillsboro: Beyond Words Publ., 2004.

"The Money of Love" e-course by Monica is a six-week adventure in financial healing, available at any time. Each week for six weeks you will be emailed a pdf lesson and mp3 meditation highlighting different aspects of financial abundance and wholeness. For more information and to register go to http://www.monicamcdowell.com/increase-your-financial-health.html

Part Seven: Of Healings and Blessings

To order my mp3 healing meditations, just visit my website at www.monicamcdowell.com.

One healer I love to recommend is Adam Dreamhealer. He has authored several books and has created two DVD's to teach people how to visualize healing. Check out his website at www.dreamhealer.com.

Photo Credits

Unless noted otherwise, photo credits listed below are attributed per agreement with Wikimedia Commons and adhere to this licensing agreement: "re-users are free to make derivative works and copy, distribute, display, and perform the work, even commercially," The rest of the photos used in this book belong to the public domain or are personal photos. If there are any corrections, please contact the author or publisher.

Turtle Totem: "KTurtle Turtle" by Michael Reschke

Introduction: "Crow in Flight" by Pheanix

Lovin' My German Non-Yoga Body: from handiyoga.com no copyright, website disabled

The Rise of the Black Madonna: "The original Black Madonna at Montserrat" by csiraf

Tibetan Mandalas and Quilting Bees: "Chenrezig Sand Mandala" by Colonel Warden

The Anti-Martha: "Mother and Daughter Paper Dolls" public domain

Why I Write: "Hildegard von Bingen" public domain

The Mowing Miracle: "Cylinder Mower Bicycle" by B. Jankuloski

Visitations: "Telephone from the 60s" by Rama

Blinded by White: "Snowy road and fields" by Ashley Dace

On Raising Intuitive Children: "Tours" by Kamel15

The Year of the Hawk: "Hawk-13" by William H. Majoros

Caveman Spirituality: "Caveman" by Isherb

The Baby with the Buddha Eyes: "Hoh Rain Forest" by Kgrr

The Secret to a Bliss-Filled Holiday: "The North Star: A Long Exposure" by LCGS Russ

The Dancing Universe: "Dance, Dance" by desicolors.com -- no copyright

Meditate Like an Otter: "California Sea Otter" by Mike Baird

Modern Day Dr. Doolittles: "African Gray Parrot in Zoo" by David De Hetre

Doggy Divine: "Meditating with Dogs" by teachingyourdogs.com – no copyright

The Trees Speak: "Talking Tree" by LasVegasVegas.com public domain under the creative commons license

Metamorphing Bears: "Resting Bear" by Rick Smit

How Sci-Fi of You: "Into Deep Space" by Serge Jadot

Glitches in the Matrix: "The Child's First Words" public domain

Irreverent Reverence: "Blue Jay" by Darren Swim

Truthiness in My Throat: "Vishuddhi Chakra" by Mirzolot2

Harry Potter, Anyone: "Magic Wand" by Martin Broz

Time Warp Travels: "G-Wave: Einstein's Theory of Relativity" by NASA public domain

I Have My Ways: "Juvenile Bald Eagle" by Sri Mesh

Gaia and the Energy of Place: "Earth" by NASA public domain

Synchronicity: "Space Needle from Below" by Kevin Noone

Eagle Eye: "Eagle Eye" by Peter Kaminski

The Sword in the Stomach: "Scramsax" public domain

A Backside Blessing: "Snoqualmie Falls" by Pavel Poliansky public domain

Energy Jell-O: "Rainbow Jello" by Mark Fickett

Angel Rain: "Here Comes Rain" by Juni

Preface: Chinese Soldiers" public domain

About the Author

When Monica McDowell is not writing (or schlepping kids around), you will probably find her working with energy: meditating on it, healing it, clearing it, intuiting it, channeling it, or frying it up in a pan. In her pre-mystic past life she worked as an ordained minister and spiritual director and served as a pastor and chaplain for several years. Monica obtained her Master of Divinity from Princeton Theological Seminary focusing on spiritual care and counseling. She has a B.A. from Seattle Pacific University graduating summa cum laude as co-valedictorian with majors in sociology-anthropology and cross-cultural communication.

Monica spent two summers overseas—one in the tribal Philippines helping to build a community center with a village—the other in Bethlehem on the West Bank working as a counselor at a Friendship Center for Jews, Christians, and Muslims. She was the founding director of Women's Sanctuary, offering inter-spiritual, inter-faith gatherings and retreats for women, and she has the distinction of being the first ordained minister ever granted civil rights in a U.S. federal ruling.

Monica lives with her husband and their two teenagers in Seattle (the city where slugs über-subsist on ever-saturated sidewalks), along with Ruffles (the dog) and Snuffles (the cat). She is most proud of the fact that she is still a sweat-pants mom in a yoga-pants mom world, and second most proud of the fact that she is known as "the walking lady" around her neighborhood and not "the crazy lady."

Connect with Monica

For more information, visit Monica's website:
www.monicamcdowell.com

Email her directly at:
monica@monicamcdowell.com
or via her website

Find her on Facebook at:
facebook.com/monica.mcdowell

Follow her on Twitter at:
twitter.com/monicamcdowell

Ordering Information

To order additional copies of this book go to:
www.monicamcdowell.com

Or, contact Synclectic Media:
www.synclectic.com

17235600R00143

Made in the USA
Charleston, SC
01 February 2013